Jack Kerouac's Nine Lives

*Three Essays By
Jim Jones*

Elbow/Cityful Press
Boulder, CO 2001

Copyright © 2001 Elbow/Cityful Press
Copyright © 2001 James T. Jones
Copyright © 1963, 2001 Jerry Bauer, photos

Individual copyrights remain with those holders. All international copyright laws apply to this book. No portion of this book may be used without prior written consent from the author and Elbow/Cityful Press.

Special thanks to: Andy Hoffmann and Karin Rathert.
The author wishes to thank The National Endowment for Humanities for its support of the research for the essay "Jack Kerouac's Nine Lives."

This book is for Nora.

First Edition
1234567890

Previously unpublished photographs of Jack Kerouac in his Northport, NY, home, 1963, by Jerry Bauer.

Cover design—Leah Peterson
Book design—Steve Creson

Library of Congress Cataloging-in-Publication Data
Jones, James T., 1948–
Jack Kerouac's Nine Lives: Three Essays / Jim Jones.—1st ed.
p. cm.
Includes bibliographical references.
1. Kerouac, Jack, 1922–1969. 2. Authors, American—Biography—History and criticism. 3. Beat generation—Biography—History and criticism. 4. Authors, American—20th century—Biography. 5. Biography as a literary form. 6. Beat generation—Biography.
I. Title.
PS3521.E735 Z7345   2001
813'.54—dc21
[B] 2001032512
ISBN 1–885089–08–2 (alk. paper)

Elbow/Cityful Press books are edited and published by
Darrin Daniel and Steve Creson.
Elbow/Cityful Press   Po Box 17261 Boulder, CO 80308
cityful@earthlink.net
www.cityfulpress.com

Contents

Introduction by Andy Hoffmann	7
Jack Kerouac's Nine Lives: A Biography of Biographies	11
Kerouactonyms	53
Kerouac in Seattle	79
Nine Lives Bibliography	93
Kerouactonyms Bibliography	100

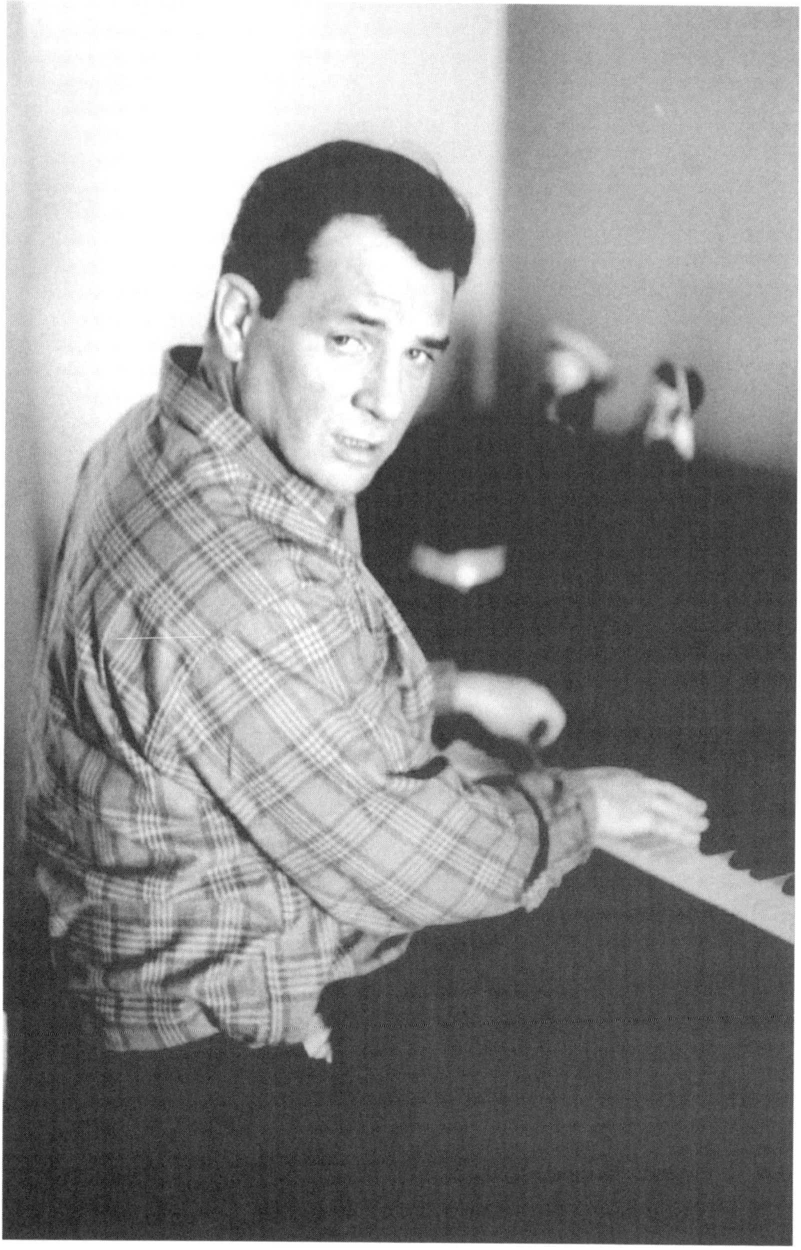

Introduction

As a leading Beat Generation scholar, Jim Jones has spent a good part of his career inspecting the autobiographical significance of Kerouac's efforts. With good reason, since nearly everything Kerouac wrote is founded in personal experience, a fact that Kerouac himself advertised well. For Jones, this grey area between the life Kerouac rendered in fiction and the life the writer actually lived has become a major concern. On one hand Jones has done more than his share to legitimize Kerouac's literary production in the face of a cynical academy, making it clear that "Kerouac's primary value lies in his ability to return relentlessly and insightfully to the events of his own life to provide the material for fiction." On the other, Jones has looked too deeply into Kerouac the man to fall into the trap of anointing him a saint.

The path for Jones has been tortuous. To date he has written four books that delve into Kerouac's work and/or life. In his first, *A Map of Mexico City Blues* (1992), Jones takes one of Kerouac's most esoteric pieces and explores, among other things, how Kerouac's split between the Catholicism of his upbringing and the Buddhism he was so freshly enamored with created a profound dialectic, the friction of which triggered a music, a poetry, an art that, as Jones states, "transforms life without falsifying it." Jones's most important contribution to Kerouac studies is *Jack Kerouac's Duluoz Legend: The Mythic Form of an Autobiographical Fiction* (1999). In this ambitious work, Jones reads the novels that make up Kerouac's Duluoz Legend using Freud's oedipal complex as a theoretical guide. Obviously, viewing literature through psychoanalytical eyes is nothing new, but the thoroughness of

Jones's study and the rigor of his analysis goes a long way towards unpacking some of the most troubling aspects of Kerouac's relationship to his family, and shows how Kerouac wove these relationships (or lack of them) into the novels.

Use My Name: Jack Kerouac's Forgotten Families (1999) started out as a biography of Kerouac's daughter, Jan, but when at the last minute she refused him permission to use a long interview that was to be the center of the work, Jones was forced to abandon the idea of doing a comprehensive portrait. While the book still focuses on Jan, it makes no claims to an exhaustive biography, and spends a good many pages on other "minor characters" who add to our understanding of what is fact and what is fiction in the Kerouac legend, and why, finally, we should be cautious about making him into a hero. *Use My Name* reads like a novel where, in the end, the writer himself becomes a character, and in the final chapter indulges in a moment of candid reflection. After admitting his confusion about Jan's sudden and complete mistrust of him, speaking directly to the reader, Jones addresses the complexity of the nature of biography:

> Whatever you find in my portrait of Jan, or the depictions of the three other women and one man who knew Jack Kerouac intimately, though, remember this. It's a picture of me too. And a picture of yourself. If you find something lacking here and there—like love—make sure the lack is in them, not in me or yourself. If I've done anything in writing their story, I've tried to do that. Tried to make sure that I'm projecting and exploiting as little as possible, no more than is absolutely necessary to conduct human business.

And so we come to Jones's fourth book, the text at hand. In this age where so many make their careers from the blood and sweat of others, where voyeuristic tendencies have become common place, Jones's warning seems especially appropriate. In *Jack Kerouac's Nine Lives,* the book of three essays which you are about to encounter, the lead piece analyzes the ten Kerouac biographies written to date, questioning to what degree each might be "projecting and exploiting." Jones as much as anybody understands that the passion for Kerouac is compelled mightily by the fact that his books are indeed autobiographical, that they do represent "real life." Biography then becomes the natural extension of the novels, and all too often, instead of the biographer exploring territory that might deconstruct the Kerouac myth created by the novels, he or she ends up perpetuating the myth to satisfy one agenda or another, obfuscating the facts. As we discover, it's all too easy for the biographer to substantiate Kerouac's life by what is found in the fiction. And for Jones, this is the crux: even if based in autobiography, Kerouac's fiction must be looked at as such. Fiction is fiction. And on the other end of things, to ignore the hypocrisy, anger, weakness and addictions that were such a big part of Kerouac's life is to ignore elements that might in fact, as Jones proves in *Jack Kerouac's Dulouz Legend,* enrich our reading of the fiction.

Jack Kerouac's Nine Lives offers bibliographical references that even the most fanatic Kerouacians will find fresh and useful. The essay on Kerouac's naming of characters should be required for anyone interested in writing a work of autobiographical fiction. In the book's final essay, "Kerouac in Seattle," Jones shows how easily legends are made, and, in an ironic twist, how difficult it is to report on Kerouac without using the fiction as a guide. In the end, however, this book does more than argue points of biographical integrity. This book speaks of Jones's own enduring passion for Kerouac as an autobiographical writer, and his desire that the whole of Kerouac's life—the vital, the sad, the ugly—be applied to the readings if this grey area is to be exposed, if the truth is to be known. In these postmodernist days, truth is a strange word. This is what Jones addresses, and maybe we should listen.

—Andy Hoffmann, Stanley, Idaho, 2001

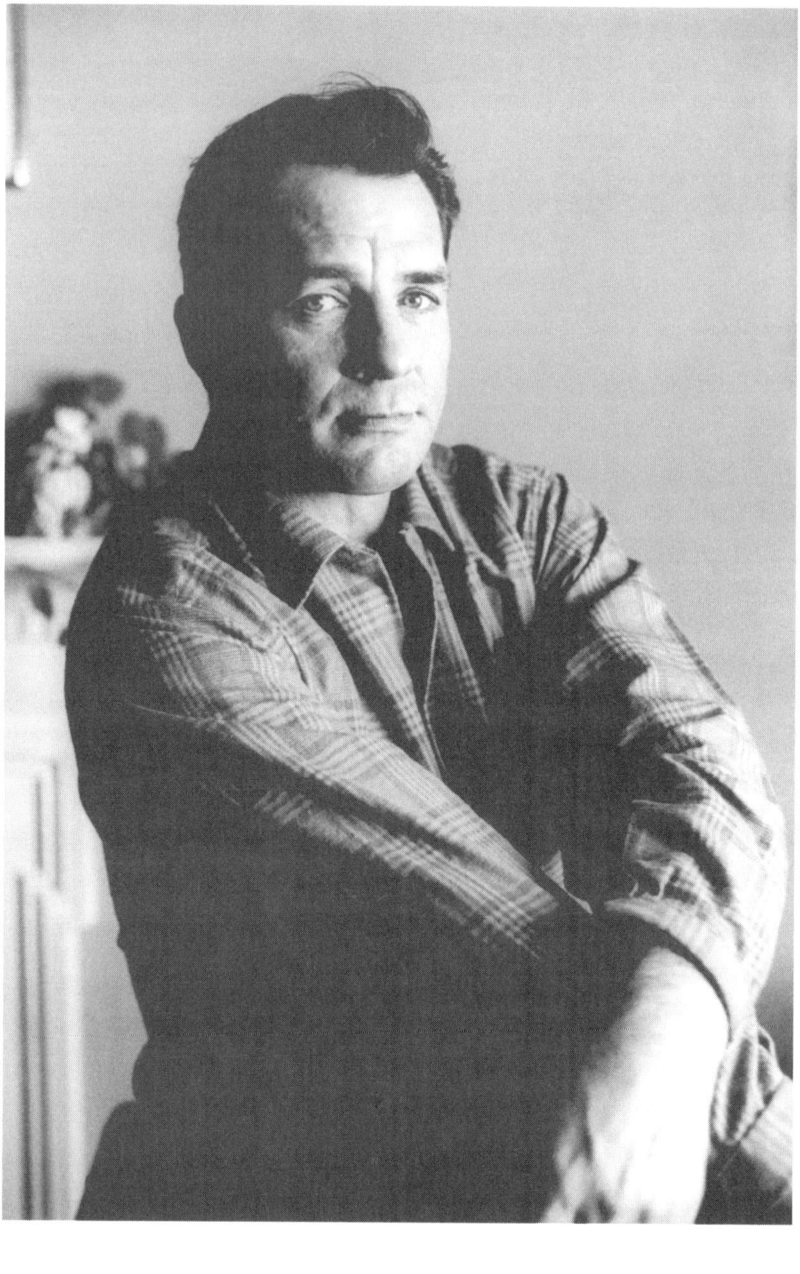

Jack Kerouac's Nine Lives:
A Biography of Biographies

...since he is a cat with at least nine lives, one of which has become an intimate buddy to literally thousands of people of our mutual generation and which we will carry with us to oblivion or old age...
—Seymour Krim, "The Kerouac Legacy"

"The criterion of a novel, a true history," Jack Kerouac noted in a journal entry in 1957, "is that it matters that there's an endless amount of information missing" (More Mexico City Blues). From 1973, four years after his death, when the first book about him appeared, to 1998, only twenty-five years later, nine biographies probed the circumstances of Kerouac's life and times in hopes of supplying the details of what is "missing" from his own accounts. And with annual sales of *On the Road* still running near a hundred thousand, some twenty of his other books currently in print, and more of his unpublished work being ushered into print, the readership for Kerouac biography is growing exponentially. Despite the intensity of biographical scrutiny, however, the range of investigation has remained fairly narrow, and the increasingly broad demand for information to supplement the reading of Kerouac's novels coupled with the limitations of the existing biographies ensures that even more studies of Kerouac's life will be forthcoming.

The conditions that create interest in Kerouac biography reach all the way back to the Romantic revolution in literature. Just a few decades after Jean-Jacques Rousseau modernized, secularized, and popularized the classical Augustinian mode of confession by revealing (and sometimes inventing) the often unseemly contradictions in his own nature and behavior, Wordsworth characterized poetry as a "spontaneous overflow of powerful emotion" or "emotion recollected in tranquility," emphasizing the expression of the personal rather than its transformation by means of artistic technique or craft. As a French-speaking New Englander, Kerouac fell heir to both British and Continental Romantic traditions. His spontaneous prose is the direct descendent of Wordsworth's theory, and the "big structure of Confession" (*Mexico City Blues* 87) that ties all his work together uses all the other Romantic writers Kerouac admired to modify Rousseau's model: Goethe, Balzac, Proust, and Thomas Wolfe.

Two of Kerouac's most formative friendships also carried a heavy burden of Romanticism. His high school friend and mentor, Sebastian "Sammy" Sampas, felt a typically Greek historical and literary regard for Byron, as well as a strong taste for the modern Romantic realism of William Saroyan, to whom he once wrote, touting his friend Jack in the letter (Sampas). Somewhat later, a younger man, Allen Ginsberg, stepped in to fill Sammy's shoes. Though his first poems were modeled on 17th-century verse, Ginsberg's mystical tendencies soon led him to a study of William Blake, and he also acquired a particular affinity for Walt Whitman's democratic celebration of himself.

Kerouac, beginning with *The Town and the City* (1950), titled for a theory of the Romantic historiographer Oswald Spengler and imitative of the style of Thomas Wolfe, developed a method of composition, an autobiographical content, and a narrative prose that make him the most prominent exponent of the Romantic tradition—both European and American—in postmodern fiction. His preference for writing about himself resonates with the residual Romantic elements of modern culture, and several generations of readers have taken pleasure in identifying with—if not actually emulating—Kerouac's Romantic heroes.

The celebrity culture of the American Century, with its origins in the star system of Hollywood and modified by the gradual acceptance of depth psychology and the recent passion for public self-revelation, has also conditioned readers' responses to Kerouac's writing. As Freud's theories helped break the Victorian silence about personal life, "sex appeal" became a part of celebrity, and audiences began to take an interest—sometimes both prurient and envious—in the most intimate behavior of their idols. After Freud's death his followers turned away from the founder's focus on the libido and began to investigate the nature of the ego, providing a psychological rationale for the growing cult of personality. The religious and Romantic confessions of the past were transformed into a therapeutic method in the free association of the psychoanalytic couch, although the repressions of Puritanism, Neoclassicism, and Victorianism were combined and redoubled in the inquisitions of the McCarthy era.

By the time Kerouac was thrust into the spotlight of celebrity by the publication of *On the Road* in September 1957, American popular culture had already begun to react against the repressive official postwar conformity by producing a series of models for rebellion, from zoot-suiters to boppers, greasers to bikers, culminating in the marketable cinematic images of James Dean and Marlon Brando. Kerouac's Gallic good looks and intense public reticence made him a natural for media exploitation. Unlike Ginsberg, however, who had worked as a market researcher in the early 1950s, Kerouac was unequipped to manage the manipulation of his own image and unable to turn it fully to his advantage. Unfortunately, when *On the Road* rose to the bottom of the best-seller list, Ginsberg, who sometimes acted as literary agent for friends, was out of the country, and Kerouac was forced to fend for himself. As Joyce Johnson reports in *Minor Characters,* her memoir of that period, he fended unsuccessfully, and the moment that should have marked the pinnacle of Kerouac's career proved instead to be his downfall.

Kerouac's celebrity had two sides. On one hand, he had been writing in relative obscurity since the publication of his first novel in early 1950, producing ten books of varying degrees of experimental form and style before *On the Road* appeared. To many Bohemian insiders his very lack of success validated his commitment to art: Kerouac refused to sell out. Paradoxically, he also worked furiously in his obscurity, not only writing novels and studying Buddhism, but also negotiating with agents, editors, and publishers to find a way to get his books accepted without the kind of compromise he felt had marred *The Town and the City*. Ironically, it was the great

Modernist man of letters Malcolm Cowley who finally ushered *On the Road* into print, largely by revising its Romantic and experimental features into a form suitable for readers with Modernist tastes.

And so Kerouac was granted his wish to be a literary figure, but in classic fairy-tale fashion, the wish produced unpredictable results. First of all, Kerouac got notoriety rather than fame, thanks to the animadversions of numerous named and unnamed critics who came forward to condemn him, not so much on account of his fiction (although that was attacked in Neo-classical terms as formless, uncrafted, and even ungrammatical), but for the rebellious lifestyle they assumed he was not only leading and describing (which he was), but also advocating (which was only partly the case). As two of his biographers point out, "The conventional popular image of the Beat Generation…would be drawn from reporting about Jack's personal situation and friends at the time that *On the Road* was published" (Gifford and Lee 172).

The effect of this vilification was itself paradoxical. Kerouac became a bête noire among conservatives and academics, and this prejudice, which extended even into the 1990s, prevented him from being anthologized, studied, or subjected to systematic scholarly scrutiny until quite recently. On the other hand, readers avid for the literary equivalent of James Dean and Elvis Presley fixed on Kerouac, taking for granted that he lived what he wrote, assuming that what was bad for conservative critics must necessarily be good for them, and taking the novelist's commitment to his art as a sanction for their own rebellious behavior. His unwilling induction into popular culture doubled Kerouac's image for biographers: in addition to Kerouac the writer, they would have to take into account Kerouac the legend, whose fame was spread not only in and by writing but also by the intractable and usually unverifiable means of word of mouth. And so Kerouac became the "King of the Beatniks," representing contradictory values for opposed groups of readers, regardless of his own fervent hope for a more substantial—and traditional—literary fame.

Beyond these general and historical reasons for interest in Kerouac's life, the autobiographical nature of his writing provokes rather than satisfies curiosity about his private life. As Roland Barthes observed in "The Writer on Holiday," "Far from the details of his daily life bringing nearer to me the nature of his inspiration and making it clearer, it is the whole mythical singularity which the writer emphasizes by such confidences" (*Mythologies* 31). Jack's own term for his autobiographical saga, the Duluoz Legend, implies a hero who is at once mythical and historical. The putative historicity of a legend, moreover, fits into a strategy to blur the distinction between fact and fiction that novelists have used ever since *Don Quixote*. Traditionally, when a novel poses as truth it ironically justifies its own existence to pragmatists at the risk of deceiving more gullible readers. More wary readers, on the other hand, besides being suspicious of Kerouac's sweeping truth claims, may also suspect that his sincere tone and his repeated avowals of frankness protest too much and therefore may actually signal omissions.

Further, Kerouac himself continually struggled to understand the confessional nature of his own writing. In *Satori in Paris* (1965), the conclusion of the Duluoz Legend, he insists that "made-up" stories are for "adult cretins" afraid to face themselves in the mirror (10). This statement implies, of course, that he himself was brave enough to stand realistic self-scrutiny, but his invocation of the pre-Romantic image of art as a mirror of nature also implies a willful naivete about both writing and reading. Kerouac believed that his own experience could be presented in what he called "visions," and yet he remained conscious—indeed, proud—of his shaping artistic hand, taking great care to distinguish his poetry and religious writings from his "narrative novels," as though poetry signified opacity and fiction transparency. Kerouac's poetics, moreover, like Stendhal's, was all about spontaneity and flow, the effort to write rapidly and without craft in order to capture experience in all its immediacy. As generation after generation of post-Romantic writers has discovered, however, while this immediacy may be simulated in and stimulated by language, the act of writing obviously attenuates it, as Shelley's "fading coal" metaphor testifies.

Kerouac's refusal to abandon the term novel, coupled with his insistence on transparency and veracity, makes special demands on his readers. "When one moves from a satisfyingly rounded novel cast as an autobiography to an autobiography cast as a satisfyingly rounded novel," as one theorist has observed, "one moves from fictional wholeness to the proclamation of fictional wholeness" (Abbot 602). Kerouac's proclamation of wholeness may actually undercut his intention by drawing attention to it. As readers wonder whether they are reading fictionalized fact or factualized fiction, the paradoxical nature of Kerouac's practice begins to reveal itself. In order to ascertain the exact nature of their act of reading, readers find themselves craving a biographical supplement. Ironically, this biographical supplement, as it grows larger and more complex, calls into question both the wholeness and the fictionality of Kerouac's writing, so that readers get trapped in a vicious circle of using biography as a test of fictionality and fictionality as a standard for biography. This paradox combines with readers' passionate subjective interpretations of the persona of the novels they are reading to create a demand for Kerouac biography that grows out of proportion even to his continuing popularity. As the literary journalist Janet Malcolm observes in *The Silent Woman*, her brilliant study of the controversies surrounding the life of Sylvia Plath, "The reader's amazing tolerance (which he would extend to no novel written half as badly as most biographies) makes sense only when seen as a kind of collusion between him and the biographer in an excitingly forbidden undertaking: tiptoeing down the corridor together, to stand in front of the bedroom door and try to peep through the keyhole" (9).

The very first written biography of Kerouac—preceding the published ones by more than a decade—was also the first academic study of his work. Bernice Lemire, a native of Lowell's French community, began her research on Kerouac's boyhood for her master's thesis at Boston College in 1961, as Kerouac's notoriety had already begun to decline. After asserting an almost complete disjunction between Kerouac the boy and Kerouac the man, she proceeds to demonstrate that many of his adult attitudes, such as his hedonism, lack of discipline, and wanderlust, are clearly attributable to his upbringing, providing along the way a good deal of social and cultural background for Kerouac's development as a writer.

Lemire corresponded with Kerouac, asking direct questions about both his life and his work, thus eliciting some valuable information about the Lowell novels (a distinction Lemire made ten years before

Bruce Cook divided Kerouac's work into "Lowell novels" and "road novels"). Jack explained in a letter, for instance, how he had split up his own personality to create the characters of the various Martin brothers in *The Town and the City* (Lemire 48). Because of her disparaging attitude towards both her subject's work and the lifestyle it represents, Lemire (probably influenced by Kerouac's "harshest critic" [26], John Ciardi, who was on the faculty of Boston College when she was a student) avoided the hero-worship that biases the first seven published studies of Kerouac's life. In addition, however haltingly, she created a viable model for comparing Kerouac's fictional accounts of his boyhood with both documents and eyewitness accounts (6), though of the published biographies only Nicosia's makes explicit use of Lemire's research.

The earliest published biographies of Kerouac were written by people who knew their subject personally, and their books function simultaneously as memoirs of their authors' association with him. There all resemblance ends, however. While Ann Charters went on to become the pre-eminent authority on Kerouac's life and works, Charles Jarvis and his book have been forgotten.

Charters, who first met Kerouac in 1956 while she was an undergraduate at Berkeley, applied her scholarly interest to him over a decade later, when she produced an annotated bibliography for a series published by the Phoenix Bookshop in New York City. Because Kerouac collaborated on it, this bibliography itself became a resource for her own and subsequent biographies. In inviting Charters to visit him in Hyannis in August 1966, he wrote tantalizingly, "I've kept the neatest records you ever saw" (Charters, *Bibliography* 11). Besides his records, Kerouac also shared his recollections of the circumstances of writing many of his books, which Charters turned into notes to supplement her own annotations. After Kerouac died on October 21, 1969, Charters attended his funeral, and the next year she also edited a collection of his poetry for City Lights (*Scattered Poems*, 1971). The biography followed within a few years, and Charters soon broadened her interest to include all the Beats, publishing two collections of her own photographs (*Scenes along the Road*, 1975, and *Beats and Company*, 1986) and editing a two-volume reference work (*The Beats: Literary Bohemians in Postwar America*, 1984). More recently she has edited both *The Portable Jack Kerouac* and the two volumes of the *Selected Letters*.

But her impressive scholarly career has not been limited to Kerouac and the Beats. Early on, she both performed and edited the rags of Scott Joplin, as well as writing a fascinating biography of the early twentieth century African-American comedian Bert Williams. After corresponding with the poet Charles Olson, she produced an academic study comparing his work to that of Melville (1968), and later she collaborated with her husband, the musicologist Samuel Charters, to write a combined biography of Vladimir Mayakovsky and Lili Brik (1979). Charters's work is even known to students of creative writing through an anthology she edited called *The Story and Its Writer* (1991).

But *Kerouac: A Biography*, which has never gone out of print, remains the jewel in Ann Charters's crown. Its release by Straight Arrow Books, the publisher of *Rolling Stone* magazine, transformed her personal involvement and scholarly research into pop culture, replete with an appendix containing Kerouac's astrological chart as cast by Carolyn Cassady. The introduction begins in the first person with her recollection of meeting Kerouac in Berkeley in the spring following the epochal Six Gallery reading in San Francisco, where Allen Ginsberg unveiled the first section of "Howl." Charters was privileged to hear him perform it again, and she recounts her argument with Peter Orlovsky, who was to become Ginsberg's life-long companion, about the poet's stature relative to Whitman. She does not mention whether she and Kerouac discussed his plans to spend the next few months as a fire lookout in Washington state, but this real-world anecdote is followed by an academic one that occurred nearly ten years later. Charters is now a graduate student at Columbia, Kerouac's alma mater, where she hears him slammed in class by Professor William York Tindall, who was primarily a scholar of British and Irish literature. Besides establishing Charters's authority as a personal witness to events, these two anecdotes set up a tension between the sneering of academics and intellectuals, whose camp she has lately joined, and the sincerity and devotion of Kerouac's ordinary readers, to whom she pledges her allegiance. Her mission as a fledgling Ph.D. will be to justify the ways of Beats to professors.

Charters pursues her goal in classic Sixties' fashion: she pleads the political relevance of Kerouac's life and work. In her acknowledgments Charters explains, "Without doubt the second most important source for the writing of this biography after Kerouac and his family was Allen Ginsberg." She recalls that "she began asking Allen questions about Jack in 1966…at a war protest benefit reading." The reader learns in no uncertain terms that in *Kerouac: A Biography* the political is personal. "Without Ginsberg's help," its author concludes, "I wouldn't have had the information or the insight necessary to write this book" (17). The poet, close friend to both the subject and the biographer, becomes the linch-pin that connects Charters to her own narrative. This dependence on Ginsberg as a source leads to a contradictory answer to the vexed question of how much of Kerouac's own writing is fiction, how much fact. From the outset Charters maintains that "everything he ever wrote was to some extent autobiographical" (15), but she never specifies the exact extent. From her other remarks, however, this extent may be surmised. Again, she brings personal relationships to bear: "Gary Snyder once told me that Jack, in his books, was 'a very accurate reporter' of events, but that he changed certain details to protect himself legally as well as to fictionalize what he wrote about himself and his friends" (15–16).

Changing the names and details to protect the innocent autobiographer from libel suits is one thing, but fictionalization is quite another. What does this term mean in the context of a biography of a novelist? Charters answers by contrast: "The most reliable source of information about Kerouac's life were the letters he exchanged with his friends" (16). She justifies this classic biographer's fallacy by using Kerouac's own aesthetic criteria: the letters "were often written five minutes after the action they describe" (16). The length of time that elapses between experience and its recording, then, provides a gauge of authenticity in writing. Romantic immediacy is at a premium for the biographer as for the novelist, but the end of the process of verification for Charters, however, is marked by a return to Kerouac's fiction, "so interested readers can follow the story of Jack's life as he wrote it in the *Legend of Duluoz*, his 'fictional' autobiography" (16).

In returning to the notion that Kerouac's writing is autobiographical, Charters has added the qualifier *fictional*, but by placing the word in quotation marks, she reverses its polarity. She makes Kerouac's fictionalization of his own life seem the merest subterfuge to satisfy publishers' attorneys. Kerouac readers are thus permanently enjoined to read his works in order to learn about his life and to read about his life to learn the substance of his works. The two-fold purpose of this reversal only comes clear in the concluding pages of Charters's biography: first, to rescue Allen Ginsberg for literary history, and second, to ensure that readers will not recognize Kerouac the flawed, self-contradictory human being in the burnished image she is now creating of him.

Charters reports that Ginsberg was "abashed and bugged" that Jack had portrayed him so superficially, that Jack never transformed him, as he had done Burroughs, Cassady or Snyder, into "a major Dostoevsky romantic character'" (359–360). The operative word here is transformed, and Ginsberg's complaint amounts to a recognition that Kerouac failed or refused to fictionalize him. In the face of this anomaly Charters simply relies on her fixed idea: "Read as historian, Kerouac was a very accurate reporter" (360). This time, however, she appends a list of exceptions: omission rather than invention of facts characterizes Kerouac's "history"; shaping by "selection of details and emphasis"; ultimately, faithfulness to the "idea and spirit of what happened" (360). These exceptions shift Kerouac's autobiography rather farther away from fact toward the realm of fiction.

Charters ends *Kerouac: A Biography* by directly contradicting her subject: "Contrary to what Kerouac thought, it was his attitude toward experience, rather than his spontaneous prose experiments, that made him legendary in his own time" (361). She had laid the groundwork for this confrontation by admitting that she has ignored interviews Kerouac gave late in his life because "Jack's statements to interviewers sometimes contradicted earlier things he said" (16). To rescue the "young Kerouac" and to create a coherent picture of him that suited her personal political agenda, Charters was forced into sophistry.

Though Ginsberg "was no doubt his most sympathetic friend and strongest literary ally in the last years," Jack was nevertheless "suspicious of Allen's 'omniscient image mania,' his politics, and his Jewishness" (360). Charters must neutralize both Kerouac's potential anti-Semitism, his right-wing politics, and his resistance to Ginsberg's relentless and brilliant promotion of himself and his fellow Beat writers.

The only way to defeat this triple threat is to reverse the poles of fact and fiction. Kerouac is not what he wanted to be, either as a writer or as a person; rather, he is what the politics of the moment require of him. And since he is dead he cannot protest. Charters proceeds to construct an imaginary group of readers who exhibit the correct reaction to her own fictionalization of Kerouac's purpose in living and writing: "his readers come away with the indelible impression that he personified the life style that he described" (360), quite the opposite of the impression Kerouac himself gives in *Big Sur* (1961), where he begins by commenting on the contrast between the image readers have of him from his earlier books and his actual present circumstances (5), a theme that recurs throughout his later novels. But to help galvanize the movement in which she was involved as she was writing in 1971 Charters needed her own fiction more than she needed her subject's: "He gave to readers a vision of freedom and spontaneity that entered directly into the young reader's fantasies because it assumed and enforced their idealism too" (361). Propaganda here poses as prophecy.

No matter that—except in his style of composition—Kerouac showed every sign of becoming a fascist in his old age, Charters has determined to preserve him by joining him with his readers in a common cause: "His books are evidence of his presence, the young Jack still alive on his pages to rush on to the next adventure so long as there are people who read the Legend of Duluoz" (367). Reading his novels, then, becomes an act of perpetuating not the gnarly, aging, alcoholic Kerouac, but the youthful, energetic, liberal Kerouac, a person who, if he ever existed, had begun to fade before Charters ever met him. Though the contradictory Jack Kerouac was as real to her as Allen Ginsberg, through her own presence she creates by the very processes she observes him using in his "historical" autobiographical novels—omission, selection of details, shift of emphasis, attention to the spirit rather than the letter of his life—a politically sanitized subject, whom she proceeds to canonize. In the Middle Ages this would have been called hagiography, the life of a saint. In the Sixties it could be justified as agit-prop, but it is not fact as that term is ordinarily understood. In any case, this first published biography established or reinforced a need for Kerouac's readers to know more about his life so they could better emulate his rebellious behavior.

Charters began writing the book in self-imposed exile in Sweden, where she and her husband had moved as a protest against the Vietnam war. When she returned to the U.S., she learned that a writer named Aaron Latham had signed a contract to produce an authorized biography of Kerouac. She wrote to Jack's widow to inquire about access to his papers, and Stella replied a few days before Christmas 1972, discouraging her from pursuing her research (Letter, Berg Collection). Stella blamed the contract with Latham on someone else's decision, but conceded that she would honor its terms despite her own aversion to the project. Twice in the letter she expresses her belief that Jack's work rather than his life should be the focus of attention. So Charters, who had already devoted more than six years of study to Kerouac, found herself locked out of his estate.

As a practical matter, she turned her work-in-progress into a celebrity biography. By foregrounding the legendary Kerouac and suppressing the documentary one, she left only herself, as biographer, and her most important informant to inhabit the world of fact. Both subject and readers are consigned to "fictional" autobiography in the act of reading the "legend" of Duluoz. And that is the "indelible" legend upon which all subsequent Kerouac scholarship rests. In the first volume of *Selected Letters*, in which she connects many of the documents with more of her own elegant prose, Charters reveals a repentant urge to fictionalize the development of Kerouac's spontaneous prose instead of his rebellious lifestyle, but twenty-five years of legendizing cannot be reversed by counter-reaction. In a new introduction to the 1994 edition of *Kerouac: A Biography*, Charters recalls a personal debt that antedates her work on Kerouac: Charles Olson, she says, "gave me a sense of history that helped shape my view of Kerouac's life" (10). Further, "Olson believed that history and mythology were central to human experience." She does not say whether the inventor of projective verse believed the two were interchangeable.

Charles Jarvis, whose nom de plume is an anglicized version of Ziavras, was a resident of the Lowell Greek community into which Kerouac married towards the end of his life. His ethnic affiliation helped put Jarvis into contact with his subject, and Charters also acknowledges Jarvis's help. Jarvis's *Visions of Kerouac*, a "rambling and idiosyncratic biography of Kerouac by one of his high school friends" (Morrow, item 281), published in Lowell the year following *Kerouac: A Biography*, suffers not only from its author's intrusiveness but also from his obtuseness. It is the kind of book that makes you write angry questions in its margins. Of the central figures in the Beat movement, for instance, Jarvis observes, "These men who sat around and tried to swamp each other with their festering psyches were the ones who were about to step up to the podium and proclaim 'a new ballgame'" (121). This kind of pseudo-literacy, while hardly unusual, is unforgivable in an academic. When Jarvis is not busy reporting his intimate conversations with the great man, whose annoyance is both transparent and understandable, he busies himself with unfounded assertions. He seems particularly anxious to defend Kerouac's heterosexuality. "Jack never saw," he avers, "homosexuality, bisexuality, or whatever other devious dimensions the (monstrous) human brain can create" (147). As we now know, thanks to Ellis Amburn, this pronouncement—like many others Jarvis makes—falls far short of the truth.

Nevertheless, *Visions of Kerouac* has its uses. The author's very obtuseness, in fact, gives one some sense of what the Lowell insider's view of Kerouac may have been. In most communities importance is gauged by wealth, a standard Kerouac disdained; art by verisimilitude, a prejudice he helped perpetuate. Most Lowellians failed to fathom Kerouac's method of converting life into art, and Jarvis is no exception. Even his wildest speculations never reach beyond the reflection of life in Jack's novels. In its critical naivete, consequently, Jarvis's biography probably comes close to the way Kerouac's work was perceived by those he wrote about in his Lowell novels.

Jarvis also reprints letters and postcards Jack wrote to his best friend of those last years, Joe Chaput, as well as one to Charles Sampas,

Jack's brother-in-law, and several to Jarvis himself. The ones to Chaput are especially revealing of Jack's need for a close male companion, even in middle age. Jarvis also transcribes conversations he had with some of Kerouac's acquaintances who became characters in his novels, a prototype of the method used in *Jack's Book*. Perhaps the most interesting of these is with Duke Chiungos, the Telemachus Gringas of *Vanity of Duluoz*. Chiungos, in fact, gives a splendid account of Jack's adolescent shyness, both social and sexual, which Jarvis cannot comprehend.

Despite his imprecision, incoherence, and inconsistency Jarvis manages to articulate some plausible theories about Kerouac's behavior, one of which involves the connection between Jack's brother, Gerard, the little saint, and Sammy Sampas, who inspired Jack in high school with his love of the poetry of Byron. Jarvis intuitively links these two with Neal Cassady (124), though he cannot quite solve the equation. He might have added Gary Snyder and, for that matter, Joe Chaput. What Kerouac sought in his companions was both the consummate devotion of a blood-brother and a certain kind of idealism. (Cassady's wild ways often obscured both these qualities.) Jarvis misses other opportunities to take advantage of his insider status. As an ethnic Greek, for instance, he was in a perfect position to analyze Stella Sampas's feelings for Kerouac. But the thought never seems to have crossed his mind. Instead, some tantalizing hints are obscured by excessive rhetoric about true love.

Frankly, analysis is foreign to Jarvis's intelligence. This biographer is at his best when he is gleefully reporting his own attempts to prod his subject into saying something important by annoying him. This tactic, which had the effect of drawing out Jack's coarseness and vulgarity, may have been a blessing in disguise, and Jarvis deserves some credit for being among the first admirers to reveal the clay feet of the idol. Otherwise, Jarvis, who goes so far as to append a psychological essay by his son (who is, granted, a far more perceptive critic of Kerouac's behavior and writing than his father), seems by turns overawed to be permitted into the presence of his legendary subject and smugly superior to Kerouac's real drunken antics. Add to this that Jarvis's position as a professor of English at the old University of Lowell (now the University of Massachusetts/Lowell) made him an easy target for Kerouac's practical knowledge of literature, and the result is a great deal of unintended irony at the biographer's expense. Paradoxically, Jarvis presents the most extreme view of the veracity of his subject's novels: "Nothing that Jack Kerouac ever wrote was fiction, was ever contrived" (83). Despite the manifest evidence to the contrary provided by his own numerous encounters with Kerouac in Lowell in the mid-1960s, the biographer here plays sycophant, converting his subject into a postmodern George Washington—a fiction writer who never tells a lie—and simply celebrates rather than verifying Kerouac's veracity.

The dedication of Barry Gifford and Lawrence Lee's *Jack's Book: An Oral Biography* suggests that the two collaborators, one now a well-known novelist and poet (his *Wild at Heart* was made into a film by David Lynch), the other a journalist, undertook their work as a corrective to Charters's and Jarvis's books. (A decade later they collaborated on a biography of William Saroyan, one of Kerouac's early literary influences.) Marshall Clements, the person named in the dedication of their unusual biography, is the foremost collector of Kerouaciana, an extremely valuable resource to biographers (Charters relied on him for both her bibliography and her biography), especially in the days before Kerouac manuscripts began to become available in the Berg Collection at the New York Public Library and the Harry Ransom Humanities Center in Austin.

But the revisionists must pass between the same Scylla and Charybdis as their two predecessors. In their presentation of long verbatim excerpts from interviews with Kerouac's friends and associates (including Ginsberg, Carolyn Cassady, Lucien Carr, and Gary Snyder, all of whom edited transcripts of their own statements), Gifford and Lee seek to avoid the temptation to shape the material they have collected into a coherent whole. At the same time they issue a warning about the misuse of Kerouac's novels as biographical resources:

> In what follows you will read again and again, in many voices, that Kerouac's novels were fiction, not reportage. It is fascinating to see the way in which real people, places and events utilized in the books, but the technical leaps and the heart-breaking beauty in Kerouac's

prose take his novels into a realm far beyond that of the reporter or diarist. ("Prologue" n.p.)

Despite their excessively reverential tone, this admirable attempt to separate the facts of Kerouac's life from the fictional account he developed out of those facts might have served as the corrective they desired, if only they had not added the next sentence: "His books are the product of a genius at recollection." Gifford and Lee immediately muddy the waters they have just attempted to clear. I am reminded here of Coleridge's distinction between the primary imagination, the secondary imagination, and the fancy. Kerouac—and this is really his most serious drawback as a novelist—obviously did not enjoy the godlike creative power of Coleridge's first faculty. All the biographers recognize that he did not invent his material. But beyond that certainty, did he embellish the facts and shape them with novelistic form or merely vividly represent what he recalled from memory?

At the conclusion of *Jack's Book*, the authors expand upon a device first suggested by Kerouac himself at the beginning of his *Book of Dreams* (4-6), observed by Lemire (67), and later reproduced by Charters in an appendix: a table that correlates character names in Kerouac's novels with the names of actual human beings who came within Kerouac's sphere during his lifetime. Gifford and Lee's character key is by far the most exhaustive (though it omits the name of Kerouac's most famous representation of himself, Sal Paradise), and many Kerouac readers I have known admit to making frequent reference to this and other similar tables (notably three drawn up by a British Kerouac collector, Dave Moore [*Moody Street Irregulars* 1980, 1981, 1986]). The use of this key to conclude a biography, however, implies that the purpose of biography is precisely to establish the connection between the real people in Kerouac's life (including himself) and their fictional representations in his novels, suggesting further that the level of fictionalization in Kerouac's writing was extremely low. As that fictional champion of factuality Sergeant Joe Friday used to announce in every episode of *Dragnet*, only the names have been changed to protect the innocent. Finally, as the use of the character key by actual readers demonstrates, the effect of *Jack's Book* turned out to be the opposite of its authors' stated intention. Instead of proving by means of the contrast between their informants' memories of events and Kerouac's representation of those same events in his novels, both the fact and the degree of his fictionalization, they provide the easiest means of reinforcing the illusion that Kerouac did nothing more than report actual events, transcribe conversations, and invent character names for real people.

At first, Dennis McNally's *Desolate Angel*, despite its melodramatic title, appears to be a departure from the three biographies that preceded his. Here is a biography undertaken by a historian with the express purpose of viewing Kerouac in the perspective of pre-and postwar American culture. At last readers will be given a context in which to understand the cultural origins of Kerouac's autobiographical impulse and thereby to gauge the degree to which he modified it by fictionalization. McNally is extremely good about providing the facts of political life in Depression-era Lowell, for example, or what movies were playing and what novels were on the best-seller list at crucial moments in Jack's life. Sometimes he even produces data to bring home a point, as when he quotes rent prices in Mexico City in 1952, when Kerouac visited Burroughs there for the second time. Knowing that the average rent for an apartment was $27 brings home the appeal of the place for the Beats.

Though McNally shares Charters's bias with respect to Kerouac's impact on the 1960s and follows her practice of using quotations from the novels to fill gaps in his narrative, he achieves a greater distance from his subject simply on account of his interest in the bigger picture. Though he does not evaluate Kerouac's works as literature, he nevertheless perceives that Kerouac's emotional and spiritual balance may constitute the crucial element for criticism. He bequeaths this element to Gerald Nicosia, who applied it with great thoroughness just four years later. Because he fails to make the most of this important perception, however, McNally's biography finally falls flat. After his touching description of Kerouac's pain-filled last decade—which McNally renders even more poignant by showing how the ground of American culture shifted rapidly under Jack's feet at the end of the 1950s—he forgets to apply the conclusion of his own penetrating analysis. Kerouac's writing, despite his valiant effort to reformulate a crucial episode of his legend in *Vanity of Duluoz* in terms of his current struggles, could not assimilate the frequent moves, the decline of his mother's health, the effects of his late marriage, and his worsening alcoholism. Jack died young because he lost his balance. By contrast, the last lines of *Desolate Angel* seem incongruously romantic: "The myths and dreams and the art remain, to disturb or inspire. Above all else, the road endures" (347). Read more than twenty years later, this conclusion demonstrates how a biographer can be blinded to his own insight by his attachment to the subject and by his consequent failure to distinguish clearly between art and life.

So while McNally does fulfill the promise of painting a broader background in which to view Kerouac's work, he fails to resolve the dilemma of the fictionality of his subject's autobiographical writing. In a letter of March 23, 1978, printed as an appendix to Robert J. Milewski's *Jack Kerouac: An Annotated Bibliography*, Allen Ginsberg, the secret hero of Charters's biography, takes McNally to task on this very issue. Regarding the duplications he finds in Gifford and Lee, McNally, and the then-authorized biographer, Aaron Latham, Ginsberg opines that these "may come from…the habit of relying on Kerouac's novelistic texts for documentation of scenes and 'quoted' conversations" (199). Ginsberg warns McNally that "smoothing" such documentary material into his own prose "gives rise to perplexity in the reader" (199). In admonishing the historian about the danger of deriving biographical facts from Kerouac's novels, the poet makes a useful distinction between fictionalization and simple subjectivity:

> In those cases you should always warn the reader…The reason is simply that Keroauc's versions were fictions based on fact, but not all identical with actual event, part thru novelistic imagination, part thru specialization of his own views. (199–200)

In the crudest practical terms, Ginsberg advises his correspondent, "You can cover your ass by mentioning where these anecdotes come from, true or embroidered as they may be" (201). It is always good for a biographer to cite his or her sources, but Ginsberg's language suggests that the actual effect of these citations, rather than authenticating the facts of the case, may simply shift the burden of interpretation from the writer to the reader.

In the course of his critique Ginsberg expresses his approval of what he perceives to be McNally's thesis: "K's struggle against opposition and incomprehension" (201), making Kerouac sound like the initialized hero of a Kafka novel. He applauds McNally's "assemblage of obstructive reviews" of Kerouac's books and relishes seeing "all those jerks lined up against the wall of historic justice on the fields of literary time" (201). The metaphor of the firing squad for reviewers is the poetic equivalent of the conclusion of Charters's book: those who resist the value of Kerouac's work are obstructionists worthy of historical obliteration. After referring the biographer to his own gloss of *Visions of Cody* in an essay called *Visions of the Great Remember*, Ginsberg faults McNally for committing the same error as Charters by slighting the "old Kerouac" and underemphasizing the last six or seven years of his writing. Ginsberg also reveals that Kerouac's old buddy Lucien Carr, a journalist, has taken the trouble to compile a list of five similarities in diction between Gifford and Lee's book and McNally's. The poet also mentions "a booklet of marginalia errors" he himself made in reading Charters (201). In addition to their reliance upon their subject's fiction, Ginsberg catches Kerouac's biographers repeating each other, even though materials to correct the misrepresentation of Kerouac's fictionalized accounts have been available since the earliest stages of the biographical process. Sometime after the publication of *Desolate Angel* Dennis McNally was hired as the publicist for the Grateful Dead, and now it appears that the same man who had the solemn duty of announcing Jerry Garcia's passing to the world already had a history of turning life into legend.

Before 1973 Kerouac's agent, Sterling Lord, must have convinced Gabrielle Kerouac, Jack's mother, that Aaron Latham, the author of *Crazy Sundays: F. Scott Fitzgerald in Hollywood* (1971) and later of the screenplay for *Urban Cowboy*, was just the man to write the "authorized" biography of Jack Kerouac. In later years, however, Stella Kerouac, following the promise of her letter to Charters, became notorious for denying access to her late husband's personal "archive," supposedly because she was offended by Charters's explicit treatment of Jack's sex life, although as the letter makes clear, her objections antedate the publication of *Kerouac: A Biography*. In a memoir in *Kerouac's Town*,

Barry Gifford recounts a visit with Stella in 1973 in St. Petersburg, Florida, in the house where Jack Kerouac died. In the course of their conversation Stella complains not about Charters's emphasis on sex, but about her misstatement that Kerouac's only sister, Carolyn, committed suicide in 1964. This inaccuracy (which Charters corrected in a later edition of her biography) embarrassed both Stella and Gabrielle because they were devout Catholics.

But something more serious than this may have made Stella resist biographers. According to her youngest brother, John, who now manages Kerouac's estate, Aaron Latham defaulted on his contract, which required him to produce a biography within five years. Though Latham failed to produce a book, he did, however, author a magazine article about an infamous murder case in which Kerouac had been involved as a material witness in 1944. Latham's article was assailed in a document created and circulated privately by William Burroughs's secretary, James Grauerholz, who accused Latham of plagiarizing his account of Lucien Carr's murder of David Kammerer from two fictional sources (Grauerholz). The first was a collaborative novel by Burroughs and Kerouac called *And the Hippos Were Boiled in Their Tanks*, which remains unpublished, and the second was Kerouac's *Vanity of Duluoz*, the last novel he wrote. To justify his claim of plagiarism, Grauerholz lined up parallel passages from the Latham article, *Hippos*, and *Vanity of Duluoz*. Regardless of its original purpose, this strategy serves in the present context not only to expose the biographer's use of fictional material, but also to connect Kerouac's fictions with an event that can be thoroughly checked against documents created by both official and journalistic sources. Inadvertently, Grauerholz created the prototype for a matrix of authenticity that can be applied both to Kerouac's novels and to studies of his life.

Though the research and interviews of which it is composed were all completed in the 1970s, the great era of Kerouac biography, *Memory Babe*, the fifth study of Jack's life, did not appear until 1983. Gerald Nicosia, who has published only an obscure account of gay hustling in Chicago and a small volume of poetry in addition to his monumental study of Kerouac (though his history of the Vietnam Veterans against the War has been announced repeatedly in the last several years), takes his title from an unfinished novel by his subject, implying that his biography serves to complete the story begun by Kerouac about his "Canadian ancestors" (21). *Memory Babe* was also a nickname given Kerouac by his teenage pals, though to my knowledge no one has ever suggested that Kerouac, like Thomas Wolfe, whom he idolized, possessed total recall or a photographic memory. But he clearly prided himself on his ability to remember details that most of his friends forgot, especially verbatim conversations, and this conviction may have also helped sway both readers and biographers that his fictions were more like facts. In his unpublished *Book of Tics* Kerouac recorded with some urgency, "I must find out what tics recall what visions," suggesting that he was trying to work out a method to control these triggers of memory. In another of his journals he includes among his four concepts of vision, the "vision of remembering" (SK–OB), suggesting that, as Allen Ginsberg recognized, his recall involved an element—even a mystical property—of transformation.

Nicosia lists the names of nearly two hundred people who contributed information to his biography (10–11), implying a much greater diversity of viewpoints than even Gifford and Lee had provided. After *Memory Babe* was published Nicosia sold the tapes (which have now been transcribed) and other materials he gathered in his research to the Mogan Library at the University of Massachusetts/Lowell, where there has been a controversy over their availability, since Nicosia failed to obtain signed releases from his informants, and the library administrators believe the institution would be liable for any misuse of Nicosia's invaluable archive (which contains the only recordings of many of Kerouac's associates). This very wealth of information, however, overwhelmed Nicosia's organizational abilities, and he was unable to create a coherent picture of his subject.

To make matters worse, he undertakes critical readings of most of Kerouac's major works. Since *Memory Babe* has no guiding principle except to glorify its subject, these readings, valuable as they are in some cases (for instance, the ten or so pages Nicosia devotes to Kerouac's book-length poem *Mexico City Blues*), appear to be simply grafted onto the biography. Nor is there any apparent continuity among the highly impressionistic critiques themselves, though the critic does make repeated attempts to persuade his readers that Kerouac remained a true Christian even in his Buddhist devotions. Despite the subtitle of *Memory Babe—A Critical Biography of Jack Kerouac*—Nicosia, who has a phenomenal memory for details himself, missed the opportunity to clear up the growing confusion about the extent of Kerouac's fictionalization of the events of his life. Instead of systematically contrasting the wealth of material he obtained from interviews and personal correspondence with those who knew Kerouac with Kerouac's own letters and the fictionalized accounts of events in his novels, Nicosia melds them all to create his own sense of fictional wholeness, falling victim to the same tendency of which Ginsberg had accused McNally.

One last point about Nicosia's book, which is now available in a new edition from the University of California Press: it does reveal something of the motives of its author's interest in his subject. Among the last few sentences of the acknowledgments, Nicosia expresses his "loving thanks to my unflagging patron, my mother" (11). In the very next sentence, he admits that his "deepest debt is to the spirit of Jack Kerouac." He ends the acknowledgments section with an enthusiastic and unacademic "Hallelujah." One of the most obvious facts about Kerouac, discernible to readers of both his fictions and his biographies as well as to those who knew him personally, was his lifelong attachment (many would say over-attachment) to his mother. It is also well known in the network of Kerouac fans and collectors that Nicosia often took his mother along to conferences and book-signings. In fact, the first time I saw him, autographing the just-released hardcover edition of *Memory Babe* in City Lights Bookstore in the summer of 1983, she was by his side. The spirit of Kerouac that Nicosia acknowledges, unlike the political one Charters invented, is, I suspect, the psychological truth of his subject's positive attachment to his mother, a spirit Nicosia felt he understood by sympathy.

Tom Clark's *Jack Kerouac*, the only biography of this subject that belongs strictly to the 1980s, is introduced by a testimonial from Carolyn Cassady, Jack's close friend and one-time lover, and also wife of his best friend, Neal Cassady. Among assorted valuable insights, such as her perception that "in Kerouac's novels there is an underlying stream of Victorian standards," she generalizes that "some facts in all the biographies fall victim to the legend" (xii). What more authoritative reference could a biographer produce than an intimate friend of his subject who assures readers that his book "draws us into Kerouac's life...in the same manner as Jack would tell the story" (xiii). Beyond such assurances, Cassady actually endorses Clark's preference for "Kerouac's own words for most of the history" over "the recollections or interpretations of those of us who knew him and whose memories can be unconsciously selective or biased" (xii). Here is an eyewitness who swears that eyewitness accounts are less reliable than the subject's fictionalization of his own doings. Cassady's rationale, of course, is that fiction is truer than life. While she admits that "Kerouac romanticized his experiences," she finds his romanticization valuable in itself. "The trick," she concludes with only a hint of irony, "is to discern fact from fiction" (xiii).

With such a sanction, however, what reason does a biographer have to worry about facts at all? Clark, one of America's most prolific—and least known—men of letters, a novelist in his own right, would seem to have every warrant to replicate Kerouac's techniques, or use his own or invent new ones, in his narrative of Kerouac's life. Like Charters, Clark was influenced by Charles Olson and produced a biography of him as well. And also like Charters, he cannot refrain from merging history and mythology. In *Jack Kerouac*, despite Cassady's assertion to the contrary, Clark creates a legend that both contravenes and complements the legend Charters had created: the legend of Jack Kerouac, the writer whose novels, as Cassady believes, are truer than biographical truth.

But if Clark fancies the techniques of fiction, he also restrains them with the causality of historical circumstance and connects them with the conditions of literary tradition. His legend finds its origins specifically in the French-speaking neighborhoods of Lowell's Little Canada (though, surprisingly, he ignores Lemire's findings), from which its hero rises to become the American Joseph Conrad (3), the writer who masters his second language better than its native speakers by transforming his personal adventures into autobiographical fiction.

A Biography of Biographies 33

Clark's biography actually profits by heightening (rather than effacing, as in Charters's case) the contrast between fact and fiction. Like any journeyman poet—and, I suspect, like Kerouac himself—Clark understands that the value of imaginative writing, even realism, lies in its departure from the facts, however slight and subtle that departure may be, and in the readers' ability to gauge it. But as a biographer he knows the difference between fictional technique and fictionalization, and he dramatizes Kerouac's struggle to become the kind of writer he wanted to be only to create that fictional wholeness that allows biography to transcend the mere presentation of documentary evidence in order to represent the mystery of human personality. In Clark's *Jack Kerouac*, the hero, rather than struggling free of the facts, struggles in light of the facts.

Angel-Headed Hipster, as its title suggests, represents a reversion to the legend of Kerouac's lifestyle. Its author, Steven Turner, Kerouac's first British biographer, shares with Charters and Jarvis the impulse to meld his own story with his subject's. Turner's odyssey, his readers learn in the first paragraphs of his introduction, combines wandering with the search for spiritual truth. Since this combination is what led to his interest in Kerouac, readers may infer that it is what Turner discovers in his subject's life. His "quest for Kerouac" mirrors a much earlier memoir of that title by Chris Challis (in turn titled in imitation of *The Quest for Corvo*, a famous Modernist study of Frederick Rolfe by A. J. A. Symons), another British admirer who took his literary interest on the road in America in order to see some of the places and meet some of the people Kerouac describes in his novels, with the effect, intended or not, of contrasting subjective fact with subjective fiction.

Turner's quest, however, is attractively packaged for postmodern readers, and while it takes great pains to introduce a few new marginal actors in the drama of Kerouac's life, its major contribution to the genre of Kerouac biography is its inclusion of several previously unpublished photographs. The photographic documentation of the literary life, which began in America with Whitman, plays an important role in the legend-making of all the members of the Beat movement. Since Viking Penguin, which published *Angel-Headed Hipster*, publishes most of Kerouac's works (with Grove Weidenfeld second in numbers, followed by City Lights a distant but important third), Turner had direct access to John Sampas, and what is essentially a glitzy photo-album will probably become the flagship biography that bears the retro-Kerouac legend into the new millennium. If there is anything to be regretted about this eventuality, it is that Turner's honest interest in Kerouac's spirituality, one of the most complex, fascinating, and least thoroughly explored aspects of his life, is cast into the shadows by the graphic fireworks of his book.

The eighth addition to the stable of Kerouac biographies was written by a man who had professional ties to his subject, and so like the earliest studies, it functions partly as a memoir. *Subterranean Kerouac* joins a string of celebrity biographies of rock stars, including Roy Orbison, Janis Joplin, and Buddy Holly, written in the 1990s by Ellis Amburn, who thirty years earlier had edited two of Kerouac's last novels, *Desolation Angels*, which Amburn gave its final form by suggesting that Kerouac combine two shorter novels into one, and *Vanity of Duluoz*, which acknowledges his empathy on the title page. Amburn's biography is by far the most sensational treatment of Kerouac's life, focusing on his homosexual tendencies, his alcoholism, and his anti-Semitism. After a quarter-century of various kinds of glorification, the age of debunking has apparently arrived in Kerouac studies, a natural corrective to decades of unmitigated adulation. Placing Kerouac in the context of queer studies sheds an entirely new light on his representation of himself, on his encounters with up-and-coming gay writers of the 1950s such as Gore Vidal, and on his many more than previously recognized homoerotic experiences. This new perspective may also undercut some of the machismo that drives the Kerouac cult, although I suspect Amburn's approach will be summarily dismissed by homophobes.

Despite his thesis, which is the most forthright statement of bias in any Kerouac biography, Amburn also runs afoul of the tendency to rely on Kerouac's fictional accounts of his life for facts. Indeed, this biographer justifies relying "on fictional works as primary nonfiction sources" and retelling Kerouac's stories "with real people's names as accurate accounts of real events" as conventions of Kerouac scholarship, using his own personal interaction with the author to validate these practices (6). But he sheds further light on the distinction between fact and fiction in Kerouac's prose by quoting from Malcolm Cowley's acceptance report for *On the Road*, in which the distinguished man of letters informed the editors at Viking that Kerouac's book was "'a narrative based on fact, but with names and events sufficiently disguised to call it a novel'" (260). Apparently, the distinction was tenuous at best, even in the mind of a man with a great deal of experience with writers and literature. Amburn also quotes an intriguing, if somewhat mind-boggling, comment of Truman Capote on this subject: "'Kerouac writes fiction nonfiction,' Truman announced, 'I write nonfiction fiction'" (335). I take this to mean that the author's intention to write fiction or nonfiction may have the opposite appearance and effect.

Amburn supplements his factionalization of Kerouac's fiction and his narration of his own interactions with Jack by providing much new information—for instance, about the actual horror of Kerouac's death—gained through interviews with eye-witnesses heretofore disregarded by biographers. As a former editor, Amburn also offers the reader valuable insight into the New York publishing industry and the editorial process itself. Unfortunately, his thesis often intrudes into the continuity of his narrative in the form of surprisingly pat judgments based largely, it seems, on the jargon of self-help psychology. While these judgments sound out of place in descriptions of the life of an author already long dead, they may serve as a warning to readers who are all too willing to romanticize Kerouac's self-abuse, but their net effect is to add an unwanted and unnecessary moralizing tone to *Subterranean Kerouac*. This tone disables Amburn's desire to appreciate and even admire Kerouac's artistry while condemning his behavior. Ultimately, Amburn's admiration for his subject as a novelist takes on the same tone of pronouncement as his moralizing, neutralizing the benefit of his biography to some extent. Readers put off by Kerouac's behavior may be unwilling to accept the fact that he is still a major novelist. Nevertheless, I find that Ellis Amburn has given the fullest and most rounded account of Kerouac's life to date.

A July 9, 1998, article in *The New York Times*, which quoted Amburn at length on Kerouac's "conflicted" sexual orientation, also announced the forthcoming publication of a ninth Kerouac biography, *Jack Kerouac:King of the Beats*, this one by Barry Miles, well-known to Beat readers as the British Marxist biographer of Allen Ginsberg and William S. Burroughs. In *Allen Ginsberg* (1989) Miles writes dismissively of Kerouac's personality, the impact of his writing, and his contribution to the postwar youth movement. Besides allowing him to score a literary hat trick, his treatment of Kerouac as a primary subject promises to expose the contradiction—if not the downright hypocrisy—of Kerouac's rebellious literary persona and his comfortable suburban life with his mother. "There is a disparity between the image and the actual man," Miles is quoted as saying (E4). This biography, by focusing on Kerouac's right-wing politics and late-life anti-Semitism continues the debunking begun by Amburn by highlighting the "old Kerouac," reversing (without rectifying) the trend begun by Charters. In his Ginsberg biography Miles's doctrinaire excesses (his contention, for instance, that Ginsberg's poetry suffered as he became more committed to Buddhist practice) were checked by his subject, who was still very much alive at the time (and who had a contract with Miles that awarded him ten percent of the author's advance). Kerouac's complicated spiritual life is lost on the materialist biographer; nevertheless, a less legendary, more realistic Kerouac emerges from Miles's portrait.

Miles seems to have been acutely aware that he was producing the ninth full-scale biography of Jack Kerouac, so he goes out of his way to emphasize the under-emphasized aspects of the previous books. As a materialist, he excels at explaining the cultural origins of Kerouac's personality and writing. For instance, Miles shows how *The Shadow* magazine contributed not only to the formation of Jack's childhood fantasies, but also how the pulp magazine prefigured his preference for rapid writing. Occasionally, the biographer goes overboard in his search for cultural connections, as when he devotes a paragraph to the influence of Breton cooking on the food Gabrielle Kerouac served at home. Still, the preface to Miles's book is probably the most incisive comprehensive analysis of Kerouac's life and work yet written.

Beyond that, Miles proves very strong on the family background of Jack's childhood friends, providing a standard (one that Lemire perceived but rejected) by which to measure Kerouac's similarity to and divergence from the Lowell norm. Early on, the biographer vows to avoid the primary pitfall of Kerouac studies, warning himself as much as his readers that "it would be a mistake to base a biography on the books" in which his subject fictionalized his own life (xv). But this charm against the curse fails quickly and completely: only ten pages into the first chapter Miles is already quoting a character in *Maggie Cassidy* to support his assertion of Kerouac's misogyny (10). This trend continues throughout *King of the Beats*, until Miles as much as his predecessors has muddled the connection—if not the distinction—between fact and fiction.

A curious feature of this book is that unlike myself, who dislike Kerouac the man but adore Kerouac the writer (or as one Northport clammer who took a few swings at Kerouac is reported to have said, as Jack "lay in a heap on the road," "I like your books, but I don't like you" [Nicosia 645]), and unlike too many fans, who adore Kerouac the man and virtually ignore Kerouac the writer, Miles seems to like neither the man nor the writer. This is odd, since he is such a good writer himself (almost as good as Ann Charters, and that is very good). His favorite book is Jack's most conventional novel, *The Dharma Bums*. While he grudgingly recognizes the value of *The Subterraneans* as the most readable representative of Kerouac's spontaneous prose, he positively disparages many of the other novels, reserving his harshest judgment for *Visions of Gerard*. Perhaps this is an excess created by the debunking spirit Miles represents, but it creates the mistaken impression that Kerouac's only value for the present and future of American culture is as a pop-culture icon. I wholeheartedly reject this view, intended or not. Kerouac's primary value—and this will be seen more easily and clearly as the image of his rebellion fades—lies in his ability to return relentlessly and insightfully to the events of his own life to provide the material for fiction. It is his ability to adapt autobiography to the marvelously flexible form of the novel that keeps winning Kerouac new readers in the new millennium, an age when, for the first time in publishing history, memoirs have begun to outnumber novels.

Lately, highly regarded pop-culture critics such as Greil Marcus (in *The Dustbin of History*) have begun to pooh-pooh the contributions of the Beats to 1950s culture, and both Amburn's and Miles's perspectives will provide ammunition for such dismissive attitudes. The fact that Kerouac was neither a homosexual (except for the purpose of advancing his literary career) nor an anti-Semite (except for the purpose of getting attention in the period of his alcoholic decline) will probably become irrelevant in the ensuing rush to smash the idol's clay feet.

Biographies of other Beat writers often give a good sense of how Kerouac fit into the scene in the 1940s and 1950s. Jack's most important literary relationship was with Allen Ginsberg, and Barry Miles, in his equally readable biography of Ginsberg, provides special insight into the personal and aesthetic relationship between Jack and Allen. Miles, as he details the course of their friendship from the moment Ginsberg walked into the kitchen of Jack and Edie's New York City apartment in May 1944 until long after Kerouac's death, is careful to warn his readers of Allen's bias:

> Basically, Allen was presenting his Kerouac: the sensitive footballer, intimate friend, and confidant from the Forties, the great genius writer who had "heart," not the anti-Semitic Kerouac who abandoned his wife and daughter to a life as a drug addict and prostitute, and who wanted to shoot all antiwar protesters. It was an idealized, sanitized Kerouac, the greatest writer in America, the Kerouac Allen always wanted him to be. (Miles, *Ginsberg* 502)

It is a measure of their friendship, and perhaps also of Jack's charisma, that Allen refused to allow Kerouac's prejudices and personal faults to destroy their friendship. Even during Jack's last years, when he did little more than harass Allen about his left-wing political activities and bait him with anti-Semitic remarks, Ginsberg held fast to his belief in Jack's right to be an individual and to express his views candidly.

Ginsberg's concern for his old pal is underscored by the fact that his purchase of a farm in upstate New York was intended not only as a hideaway, but also "to get Kerouac to the farm to dry out" (412). Perhaps Allen also had some idea that if Kerouac dried out, especially in the remote environment of Cherry Valley, they might be able to discuss his reactionary attitude toward the social upheaval of the 1960s. At any rate, the plan failed. Still, when Kerouac finally drank himself to death on October 21, 1969, Allen began immediately—the very next day at a reading at Yale—to memorialize him. Besides reading the "211th Chorus" of *Mexico City Blues* ("I wish I was free / of that slaving meat wheel / and safe in heaven dead") and chanting the *Diamond Sutra*, Jack's favorite Buddhist text, Allen also fielded questions from the Yale audience about Jack's importance in the light of his politics. According to Miles, Ginsberg told the students in New Haven "that Kerouac had tried to follow the implications of his sad-comic view of things to the bottom of his own nature, and transcribe it in its own onrushing spontaneous flow, and leave it there for others" (427).

Later, Ginsberg made two other major tributes to Kerouac's memory and stature as a writer. The first came in the summer of 1974, when with poet Anne Waldman he founded the Jack Kerouac School of Disembodied Poetics under the aegis of the Naropa Institute. Despite some controversy over the authoritarian behavior of Naropa's founder, the exiled Tibetan Buddhist spiritual master Chogyam Trungpa, the Poetics Department has probably done more to disseminate Kerouac's ideas than any other institution. The second memorial to Kerouac organized by Ginsberg was an international conference held in Boulder in 1982 to commemorate the twenty-fifth anniversary of the publication of *On the Road*. The idea came to Allen after the success of his twentieth anniversary reading of "Howl" at Columbia in 1976 (Miles 501). Beat writers, members of the circle, scholars, students, and reporters—more than five hundred participants altogether—attended the conference, which, if it did little for Kerouac criticism, served to unify the various interest groups and remind the nation of Jack's place in postmodern literature and culture. As Ginsberg noted, the many "delicious orgies of nostalgia" led to "no great revelations re Jack K...just praised his heart and prose" (503).

What Miles captures in *Allen Ginsberg: A Biography* is the praise for Jack's heart and prose as it came over the course of nearly forty years from his most enthusiastic friend, promoter, and defender. Ginsberg was fond of saying that he owed all his poetic skill to Kerouac. What Miles makes plain is that, while this may be a typical bit of Ginsberg hyperbole, its truth lies in the two writers' shared vision of candor, spontaneity, and awe, the vision they called at the outset of their association the "New Vision," in imitation of William Butler Yeats's mystical treatise. Miles himself, while remaining strictly objective about Kerouac, allows Ginsberg's great love for Jack—and Jack's writing—to shine through. From the perspective of a biography of Kerouac's friend, it is easy to see how Ann Charters, in relying on Ginsberg as her main source, came to write the kind of hagiography that characterizes her much earlier work.

At first glance, David Sandison's *Jack Kerouac: An Illustrated Biography*, the tenth contribution to the genre, seems innocuous, a coffee-table condensation of the facts into a single column of text running on only about two-thirds of its 160 pages, a handy summary for busy urban professionals. In the actual reading, it appears superfluous, adding only a few photos of Jack in later life to the published archive, and relying heavily on Carolyn Cassady's minor revisions to the record. Even her introduction, which puts Sandison second in line after Tom Clark, begins on a weary note, asserting that the flood of books on Kerouac issues from the crass needs of "ego boost or just plain cash" (10). (Surely Cassady herself has felt those needs as acutely as any of us.) She asserts further that Sandison's book is an exception. Unfortunately, it is more an exemplar than an exception.

Cassady intelligently observes that Kerouac's "consistent inconsistency" beguiles his readers into projecting our own interpretations on both his motives and the meaning of his works. Of course, that is what all good writers do. That is why literature, including Kerouac's, makes use of myths and symbols. These are the Rorschach blots that enable us to find our own images in his life and writings. In fact, Sandison concludes his commentary by arguing that Jack's books continue to sell because they "still provide satori for generations who were not yet born when Jack first set out to capture and recount the rebellious spirit of his times" (157). It is Sandison's consistent inconsistency that renders his book superfluous. Its analysis is superficial, it takes no stand (other than a few half-sneers at academia—always an easy target), and it offers no new insight into either Jack Kerouac's life or his works.

If it simply satisfied itself with mediocrity (and what other reason besides "just plain cash" could there possibly be for writing or publishing such a facile treatment of an author who now annually elicits several books with far more serious, sensitive, and stylish approaches than Sandison's), *Jack Kerouac: An Illustrated Biography* might be forgiven its superficiality. But under the aegis of Cassady's implication that this author understands the era in which his subject "lived his formative years" (10), and taking his cue from Steven Watson's cultural history of the Beat generation, Sandison merely creates the illusion of understanding the world in which Jack came of age. He does this largely by reproducing photos of each period (many of which are unidentified) and by the use of souped-up graphic design (many of the elements of which, instead of emphasizing passages in the text, often make it impossible to follow).

Sandison's use of British terminology (e.g., "saloon" for family car) will not only confuse American readers, but will also undermine his authority as a commentator on American culture. At one point he has Kerouac and his English buddy from prep school, Seymour Wyse, taking in baseball games at Christmas time (41), and later he follows Jack and Neal's drive to Mexico City (the one recounted in the fourth section of *On the Road*) along Interstate 35 (76). While these and many other minor factual errors might be excused if so many resources did not exist (and Sandison had easy access to one of the best human ones, the British Kerouac scholar Dave Moore, who has spent his life providing the kind of background information Sandison cavalierly ignores), they pale beside the author's attempt to disguise his own laziness in journalese. The false excitement of Sandison's prose (San Francisco in 1956 is "abuzz with all things Beat" [108]), its exaggerations and imprecisions (Gabrielle Kerouac's influence is a "curmudgeonly omnipresence" [87]), and its complete lack of modulation reverse the effect he intends in his conclusion. Rather than demonstrating the reasons for the continuing interest in Jack Kerouac's life, Sandison gives the impression that the facts have suffered cardiac arrest and that his electrifying style has been called in to jolt them back to life. Too late. Under his crude treatment, rigor mortis has already set in.

It is probably no accident that in the last sentence of his book Sandison implicitly compares Jack Kerouac with Ronald Reagan. Perhaps subconsciously he has gained some insight into Kerouac's late-life reactionary rhetoric. Consciously, however, Sandison fails to notice even in his own sparse quotations that after the publication of *On the Road* Kerouac was reviled by both the right wing (*Time*) and the left (*The Nation*). I suppose that to the biographer of Che Guevara, Sharon Stone, Robert Maxwell, and Ernest Hemingway, one form of communication is the same as the next. But to call Jack Kerouac "a great communicator" is to damn him by faint praise. Better dead than two-dimensional.

Fortunately, a real revolution is about to occur in Kerouac studies. The scroll version of *On the Road*, now on deposit in a custom-made container (dubbed "the world's most expensive toilet-paper holder" by the conservators who made it) at the New York Public Library and sold in May 2001 to a Baltimore millionaire, will someday be unrolled (perhaps for the last time), photographed, and published, hopefully in facsimile (though probably not as a scroll). Its one-hundred-foot-long paragraph, employing the actual names of the people and places depicted, will provide a new and perhaps definitive standard by which to measure the degree and kinds of fictionalization in all Kerouac's published novels. It may also become possible to attribute various fictional devices, some to publishers and their lawyers, some to editors, some to Sterling Lord, and some to Kerouac himself. The second volume of Kerouac's *Selected Letters* was published in the fall of 1999, but the storm of criticism that greeted the appearance of the first volume did little to ensure that its editor, Ann Charters, took more care in explaining her criteria for selection, omission, and deletion of material. Douglas Brinkley, author of *The Majic Bus* and highly acclaimed historian and biographer of Jimmy Carter, has recently become the second person appointed to produce an authorized biography of Kerouac, and excerpts from Jack's journals edited by Brinkley have already appeared in *The New Yorker* (June 22 & 29, 1998) and *The Atlantic Monthly* (November 1998). Brinkley wrote to me in May 1999 to say that he will model his book on David Donald's *Look Homeward: The Life of Thomas Wolfe* and Garry Wills's *John Wayne's America*, suggesting a combination of literary and popular culture biography.

Kerouac's own record of his daily life, compared with, say, his four published accounts (one a sequence of poems) of his summer on Desolation Peak in 1956, will show how he manipulated this raw material to suit the different contexts of *The Dharma Bums, Desolation Angels, Lonesome Traveler,* and "Desolation Blues." The principals in Kerouac's life, including William S. Burroughs and Allen Ginsberg, whose "omniscient image mania" so offended the aging Kerouac, have begun to die off, so future biographers will be forced to rely more heavily on documentary sources, just as the constraints caused by the potential for libel begin to loosen. The lawsuit filed by Jan Kerouac in May 1994 to gain a portion of her father's multi-million-dollar estate seems to have petered out, especially after the New Mexico State Supreme Court in September 1999 refused to overturn an appellate court decision that Gerald Nicosia, as her literary executor, has no right to pursue it on her behalf.

All these factors, added to the increasing distance in time from the events Kerouac lived and described, will soon make it far less likely that his biographers, as Ginsberg once observed, will be "so overwhelmed by his own narratives that they borrow his elan & method too literally & attempt to complete, rival or parallel him..." (Milewski 201). Rather, as I have come to believe, future students of Kerouac's life and work will find that, to appropriate Lytton Strachey's view of Florence Nightingale, in the real Jack Kerouac's life "there was more that was interesting than in the legendary one; there was also less that was agreeable" (135). When the agreeability of Jack Kerouac's legend, either as a rebel or a writer, ceases to matter to biographers, objective biography can begin to counterbalance the previous romantic image. Despite their excesses and their limitations, *Subterranean Kerouac* and *Jack Kerouac: King of the Beats,* take the first steps in that direction.

A growing number of memoirs also promise greater objectivity in future treatments of Kerouac's life. Joyce Johnson's dramatic juxtaposition of her own relationship with Kerouac and her ill-fated friend Elise Cowan's relationship with Allen Ginsberg, along with Carolyn Cassady's mother's-eye view of her husband's numerous escapades with Kerouac in *Off the Road*, has provided the foundation for a substantial feminist critique of Jack's life. Jan Kerouac's autobiographical novels, *Baby Driver* (which appeared in a new edition in the summer of 1998) and *Trainsong* (also available in a new edition), detail the child's attempt to compensate for the total absence of her father. *Nobody's Wife*, the recollections of his second wife and mother of his only child, Joan Haverty Stuart, was published in 2000 by Creative Arts in Berkeley, the same publisher that brought out Carolyn Cassady's *Heartbeat. You'll Be Okay*, the memoir of Kerouac's first wife, Edie Parker, exists in a rough draft.

Stephen Edington, a Unitarian minister in Nashua, New Hampshire, who conducts tours for Kerouac fans, has written a thirty-thousand-word history of Kerouac's family called *Kerouac's Nashua Connection*, published by Transition Publishing in 1999. Though full of valuable research, Edington's book—perhaps inevitably—often reads like the "begat" verses in the book of *Genesis*. While it helps straighten out many of the inaccuracies regarding Kerouac's relatives frequently reproduced in the previous biographies and provides excellent photos of places associated with the family, only the most avid Kerouac fans and the most diligent Kerouac scholars will be able to generate the interest to read it.

Perhaps before it is too late, Edington or someone else will begin to investigate the lives of Kerouac's mother and sister, which were so characteristic of their different eras. Paul Maher, editor of the latest Kerouac fanzine, *The Kerouac Quarterly*, is currently circulating a proposal for a book called *The Seeds of Galloway: Jack Kerouac's Lowell*, which would certainly be an appropriate place to expand the family narrative to include the Kerouac women. Maher can also flesh out the photographic sketch of Kerouac's hometown provided by John Dorfner's *Visions of Lowell*. Tony Sampas, the nephew of Kerouac's teenage pal Sammy, has unearthed the published and unpublished writings of his uncle, a medic who died from wounds he suffered at Anzio in World War II, and perhaps someday he will find time to turn his attention to the life of his deceased Aunt Stella, Kerouac's third wife. My own book, *Use My Name: Jack Kerouac's Forgotten Families*, sheds light on Kerouac's relations with his three wives, as well as on his relationship with his nephew, Paul Blake Jr., and his lack of relationship with his own daughter. But there is much more work for future biographers here, too.

Gore Vidal's *Palimpsest*, which Amburn cites in *Subterranean Kerouac*, provides an antidote to the heterosexist bias of most Kerouac biography, joining other memoirs by Kerouac's associates, such as Neal Cassady's *The First Third*, Herbert Huncke's *Guilty of Everything*, and John Montgomery's *The Kerouac We Knew*, which give readers the perspective of those who have been fictionalized by Kerouac in his novels. At least two people have been amassing information about Neal Cassady's life, both before, during, and after his association with Kerouac, to supplement William Plummer's *The Holy Goof*, and as Kerouac's literary reputation finally supersedes—or at least outlives—the lingering negative image of his irresponsible behavior, more and more of his friends and acquaintances in later years are coming forward to tell their stories, as in the collection of Florida anecdotes in *Kerouac at the Wild Boar*.

Jim Christy's *The Long Slow Death of Jack Kerouac* represents a more personable—and better written—version of Brad Parker's *Kerouac: An Introduction*, providing a summary of Kerouac's life and thumbnail critiques of his novels. Like any true fan, Christy takes Kerouac's greatness for granted, characterizing it as a form of Catholic mysticism and dismissing out of hand the contemporary critiques of Jack's works. Christy's hero-worship leads him to the inevitable fallacy: the Romantic (and also Modernist and New Critical) notion that any kind of obnoxious behavior on the part of a writer can and should be excused by his devotion to art. Nevertheless, Christy adds new bits of biographical information—particularly about Jack's ethnicity and his later years in Florida—as well as bits of autobiography. We learn from him, for instance, that Kerouac's stamina for drinking, writing, and living persisted to the bitter end, at the same time we learn that Jim Christy was selling caramel corn in Clifton Heights, Pennsylvania, when he first read *On the Road* (characterized as a pot-boiler later in the book [94]).

Christy is also obviously an expert on Beatsploitation: he gives terse critical summaries of Hollywood's attempts to sensationalize, if not vilify, Kerouac and the Beats. But protective portrayal of Jack as a victim of an uncomprehending society prevents Christy from estimating the true value of such satirical attacks. If anyone victimized Jack Kerouac it was Jack himself. If he had been able to respond to these attacks for what they were—a disguised attempt to domesticate, co-opt, and mainstream him and his kind—he might have won the literary canonization he so desired far sooner. But Kerouac—like Christy—seemed unable to laugh at himself. And Christy is less like Kerouac and much more like the other Kerouac biographers he despises—Charters is "the worst," Nicosia the best (but with serious reservations, of course)—than he can recognize, seeing himself in his subject, personalizing, as he says, both Jack's life and his works (33). He leaves the impression that no one understands Jack Kerouac or his writing except Jim Christy. But a writer of a biographical book saying he is not a biographer is like a person running for political office saying he is not a politician.

Perhaps because Christy's own rebellion seems to have also taken a literary turn, he observes of his exemplar, "Jack Kerouac wasn't a rebel, he was a cultural revolutionary. Rebels are committed to what they are rebelling against, want parents or town, country, college, or peers to take notice of them, to shake a finger, acknowledge their rebellion, say the sorries, and accept them back into the fold" (85–86). To my mind, a more accurate description of Kerouac's desires could hardly be conceived. Because he was so committed to literature, when he didn't get the serious admiration he wanted from parents, town, country, college, and peers, he simply went to pieces. But if Jack Kerouac—or Jim Christy, for that matter—can thumb his nose at society, why can't society thumb its nose at him? In pure point of fact, a cultural revolutionary also depends on the culture he is revolutionizing, and the last thing a revolutionary wants is a soft target. Finally, Jim Christy and others of his ilk should face the fact that it was Kerouac's vilification by the media that made him into a cult figure and augmented the fame he enjoys today. That which did not kill his reputation has made it immeasurably stronger. Later rather than sooner, but finally, after all, he got what he always wanted: he has been subsumed into the mainstream, just like those of us lesser rebels who now write books—whether as "the completion of an assignment" or "a job of work" (107) or for the sheer hell of it—about him. If it is difficult to remain a rebel when you are middle-aged, it is impossible to remain a revolutionary long after you are dead.

Numerous Kerouac fans are working on many other aspects of his life (though paradoxically, those who know most about the details of Kerouac's life and writings seem unwilling or unable to write book-length studies). Roger Brunelle, a native of Lowell's French community, though a generation younger than Kerouac, has extended Bernice Lemire's ground-breaking work by tracking down the records of the nuns who taught Kerouac in grade school, archived in their motherhouse in Quebec, as well as translating Kerouac's French writings, but Brunelle will probably save his findings for a literary retirement project. The eminent British Kerouac scholar and founder of *The Kerouac Connection* (now being edited in the U.S., after a lapse of several years, by Mitchell Smith), Dave Moore, has prepared a reference book called *The Kerouac Companion*, which relates the people, places, and incidents in Kerouac's fiction to their sources in real life. If and when Moore's book finds a publisher, it will provide an invaluable tool for verifying the accuracy of the biographies, as well as a handy gauge for measuring the degree of fictionalization in Kerouac's novels. John Dorfner has already published two informative little books about Kerouac's haunts in Lowell (*Visions of Lowell*) and in Rocky Mount, North Carolina, where he often stayed in the 1950s with his sister, her husband, and their son (*Visions of Rocky Mount*). Charles Shuttleworth, a young teacher at Horace Mann, the prep school on the northern edge of New York City that Kerouac attended in 1939–40, has compiled valuable information on Jack's time there, including a collection of his earliest writings as well as reminiscences of his classmates.

Maps of Kerouac sites in and around Lowell have been produced, and the annual Lowell Celebrates Kerouac! festival held every year on the first weekend in October provides not only a gathering place for Kerouac fans but also a venue for the exchange of academic criticism. In May 1998 I gave a lecture on "Jack Kerouac in Seattle," after which someone suggested that I could take the same approach to many cities: San Francisco, Denver, Mexico City, New York, Tangier, even Paris.

The possibilities are limited only by the imagination of the researcher and the subject's itinerary, since the interest in Kerouac's life seems to be insatiable.

While the genre of documentary film and video has not added much new knowledge of Kerouac to the biographical record, it helps satisfy the craving of Kerouac fans for a more dramatic treatment of Jack's life, a craving also nourished by numerous stage performances, most notably Vincent Balestri's one-man show, *Kerouac*, which has been playing around the U.S. since the early 1980s. Films have also given audiences an opportunity to see many of the principals in Kerouac's life, judge their characters by appearance and demeanor, and thus evaluate more accurately their biases.

What Happened to Kerouac?, most of which was filmed during the 1982 Naropa Institute conference to commemorate the 25th anniversary of the publication of *On the Road*, pretends to no purpose other than to present those who knew the subject, including rare footage of Kerouac's only child, Jan. A "profile" aired on Bravo in April 1998, by contrast, argued the thesis that Kerouac's nine weeks as a fire lookout in 1956 marked the turning point in his life. Films like *Kerouac* and the long-awaited *Go Moan for Man* by Doug Sharples (which finally premiered in October 1999 after seventeen years in the making—the same length of time it took Joyce to complete *Finnegans Wake*) attempt to dramatize incidents in Kerouac's life, usually with disastrous—that is, ludicrous—results. To give him his due, Sharples does attempt to balance his dramatization with both archival footage, interviews with Kerouac's associates and later critics, shots of significant locations in the author's life and writings, and readings from his work.

As Hollywood continues to discover (after *Heart Beat*, a sincere effort to turn Carolyn Cassady's memoir into a feature film in 1981, and the perhaps equally sincere but even less successful *The Last Time I Committed Suicide* [1995], based on Neal Cassady's memoir), dramatic homages to the Beats are apt to fall flat. That is probably the reason that Francis Ford Coppola, who has owned the movie rights to *On the Road* for over twenty years, delayed starting production of the film until 2001. Oddly enough, *The Subterraneans* (1960), the only film version of a Kerouac novel to date, presents a surprisingly accurate account of the tensions in his life in 1953, once the elements of "Beatsploitation" are discounted.

In a new preface to his venerable critical study, *Kerouac's Crooked Road*, Tim Hunt, one of the first readers to affirm Kerouac's fundamental literariness, has suggested the possibility of applying postmodern modes of criticism to judge Kerouac's writing (xxv-xxvi). The same is true of Kerouac biography. Ann Charters has already begun to fulfill Tom Clark's failed promise to understand Kerouac's life and writing as an assimilation tale (Charters, *American Authors*), and a full-length treatment in this perspective will inevitably address Kerouac's class origins as well as his presentation of the voices of the marginalized and disenfranchised in his writing. Given recent interest in Buddhist studies, someone is also bound to expand Steve Turner's study of Kerouac's spirituality.

Before any further serious biographical or critical study can be undertaken, however, an immense amount of textual scholarship remains to be done. This most tedious aspect of literary research has too long been forestalled both by Kerouac's bad reputation in academia and his status as a pop-culture figure; however, both biographers and critics need to know not only his published words, but also what he intended to write and actually wrote in his journals, letters, poems, marginalia, manuscripts, typescripts, and corrected galleys. A formalist critic like Hunt recognizes the crucial dissonance of Kerouac's "attempts to create simulacra...while yet searching for a style and sense of writing that would both capture and create authenticity" (xxvi). For both critic and biographer, then, the relation between fictionalization of content and authenticity of style, which has bedeviled all the studies of Kerouac's life, will continue to present problems, but these problems can be solved progressively without recourse to absolute constructions of the nature of fact.

First, if Kerouac is to be taken seriously as a literary figure, his work must be prepared by textual criticism. Once the authorized texts have been determined by reference to Kerouac's manuscripts and to his stated intentions in journals and correspondence, the best biographies of the very autobiographical writers Kerouac most admired

(James Joyce, for example, whose life and works present many of the same difficulties as Kerouac's) can serve as models for future studies that appreciate the value of his work by illuminating the nature of his character. When all the parties involved come to accept that they must compare all the relevant information about his life with all the pertinent passages in his writings to create the most plausible realistic picture of Jack Kerouac's life, the conditions will be ripe for the creation of "the newest manifestation of the same old dreary mystery of personality" (*The Subterraneans* 100). This manifestation, whether it be Douglas Brinkley's or someone else's, will undoubtedly be the most accurate and therefore the most useful version of the legend of this American literary icon. However, if it fails to provide a rationale for using biographical information to appreciate the formal qualities of Kerouac's poems and novels, it will simply add to the existing poverty of riches. No matter how many biographies of Jack Kerouac are produced, the record will remain incomplete until a biographer explains to the widest possible audience—fans, critics, academics, journalists—how the facts of Jack's life help us gauge his achievement and stature as a writer. That is, until biography is placed in the service of art.

In a 1986 essay on William S. Burroughs, the poet Alan Ansen, who appears under various character names in five of Kerouac's novels, asks the sixty-four-dollar question: "Why so much biography in the discussion of a literary figure" (10–11). Part of his answer applies as well to Kerouac as to Burroughs: "…Because…writing is more than a matter of cerebrally selective craftsmanship, is, in fact, the total and continuous commitment of a given history, the raw materials of that history have public importance and back up the testimony of that work" (11). Raw materials and testimony may constitute a mixed metaphor, but the two terms characterize perfectly the relationship—and the ratio—between Jack Kerouac's life and work, a relationship that all future biographers would do well to bear in mind. The Duluoz Legend represents "the total and continuous commitment" of Kerouac the artist to the history he both acted and suffered.

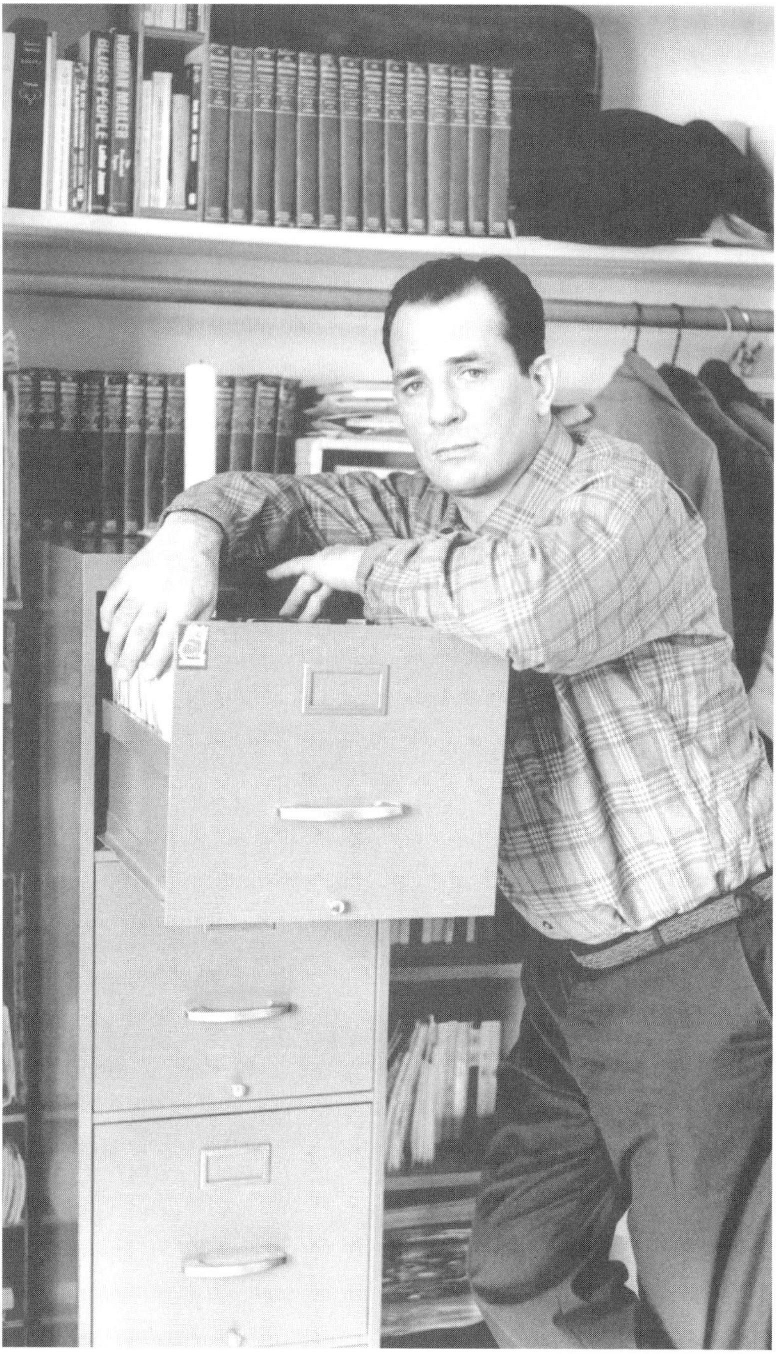
BLUES PEOPLE
NORMAN MAILER

Kerouactonyms

One

In September 1987 I took a group of students to Lawrence, Kansas, to attend an event called the River City Reunion, where many of the writers associated with the Beat movement were scheduled to appear. Early in that long weekend, one of the most personable and outgoing of these students met and befriended Jack Kerouac's first wife, Frankie Edie Parker, the woman who actually brought Kerouac, William S. Burroughs, and Allen Ginsberg together in the mid-1940s.

At some point, Edie gave him a copy of a small press edition of an excerpt of her memoir, *You'll Be Okay*, which remains unpublished in its entirety. When she autographed the pamphlet, she subscribed beneath her own name the names of several characters in her former husband's novels that she took to represent herself. Among these are two characters—Judie Smith and Edna Parker—that scholars generally accept as Jack's thinly veiled representations of Edie in *The Town and the City* and *Vanity of Duluoz*, the first and last novels published during his lifetime, both of which cover the brief period of their love affair and marriage (1942–1946); one character—Elizabeth Martin—that no one, I believe, suspected of having been modeled on Edie; and two names—Ella and Emma—I have been unable to locate in any of Kerouac's writings (though a character named Elly is mentioned in *Visions of Cody)*. She missed an allusion to her under the name of Marie in *The Subterraneans,* and in an unpublished collaboration with William S. Burroughs called *And the Hippos Were Boiled in Their Tanks* she appears as Janie.

Edie's recognition that something of herself is reflected in all these characters raises some fundamental questions about the nature of fictionalization and draws attention to Kerouac's naming process, which helps structure his avowedly uncrafted autobiographical novels.

Character names, charactonyms or personanyms as they are sometimes called, though they seem at first to be relatively artificial, play a crucial role in the creation of fictional characters. While character itself consists of a number of variables, as Baruch Hochman points out in *Character and Literature* (89), literary names "correlate with social practice" both in terms of the cultural significance of family names and in the choice of given names and nicknames, functioning as "a kind of limited scenario writing" (27). Character names fall into two basic categories: the realistic and the poetic. In the first category, the teller of the tale chooses either an actual name or a name that would be understood by the audience as a possible actual name to represent a character, as Kerouac chose Judie and Edna to substitute for Edie (and as Edie herself apparently misremembered Ella and concocted Emma). In legends such names are often the same as those borne by the actual human beings upon whom the fictional characters are modeled, lending the stories in which the characters appear an air of authenticity, which partly explains Kerouac's desire to use his friends' real names in his writing, since he affected to write the legend of his own times—the Duluoz Legend.

The paradox of using real names to create verisimilitude in fiction cuts to the very heart of fictionalization. At least since the beginning of the novel the realistic naming of characters has taken on this dual, if not contradictory, function, for the novelist's quixotic desire is to name characters in such a way as to mark them as both mimetic and semiotic, representations of the real and replacements for the real, in other words, as both memories and experiences. Kerouac epitomizes this contradictory impulse (which in turn appeals to the confused desire of American culture to restrict the imagination to the realm of the real), and his preference for the real-life names of the models for his characters bespeaks both his naive faith in the transparency of writing and his confidence that style would distinguish his fictional characters from those found in conventional newspaper and magazine reporting.

Kerouac apparently believed that a reliance on reportage would help him avoid "craft," which he viewed negatively, and this marriage of fictional technique and factual content makes him one of the fathers of the New Journalism.

After the industrial revolution, as news came to compete more directly with fiction for the time and attention of readers, the naming of characters, an area in which only the novelist has much leeway, reflected the changing social uses of fiction. At first, novelists clung to poetic charactonyms, perhaps to distinguish their characters immediately from those in the broadsheets being cranked out by the tens of thousands each day on the newly invented steam presses. For models for their new naming practices Victorian writers still reached back to the etymological derivations of biblical personages, the stock characters of Roman drama, or the allegorical figures of the Medieval miracle, mystery, and morality plays, as Kerouac recognizes through his narrator in *Desolation Angels*. Duluoz, upon being introduced to an old carpenter (whose real name was Oscar Banner), exclaims in an aside, "Mr. Winter (Ah Anthony Trollope)" (93, parentheses in original; there is no Mr. Winter in Trollope, though there is a character named Mr. Winterbones). Yet Kerouac also sometimes resorted to allegorical names, if only to express his displeasure with the necessity of renaming the originals. With the rise of realism in the late nineteenth century, fiction and journalism grew together again, as the practitioners of the latter craft gravitated to the former, and realistic names naturally gained preference over poetic ones.

As a curious example of how ontogeny may rearrange phylogeny in art, Kerouac began with a typical realist naming process as he wrote *The Town and the City* in the late 1940s, progressed to a total rejection of this process in favor of using actual names when he discovered his method of spontaneous composition in 1951, compromised with publishers for the next fifteen years by inventing more amusing naming processes of his own, and ended when his authority and lack of popularity combined to allow him to use real names in *Satori in Paris*, the book that concludes the Duluoz Legend. In a sort of fictional postscript, however, Kerouac returned in his last novel to the same material as his first, opting to use the "pantheon of uniform names" he had first envisioned for his characters in 1961 in the preface to *Big Sur* (n.p.). But in *Vanity of Duluoz* he sometimes consciously muddies the water of his naming process by revealing the true identity of the fictional character even as he conceals it, as when the narrator suggests that the renaming of a mountain in Greenland after himself and his friend Duke—"Mt. Duke-Duluoz"—should be read as a substitute for "(Mt. Ford-Kerouac)" (104, parentheses in original), or that the mispronunciation of Duluoz as Du Louse actually stands for the mispronunciation of Kerouac as "Ker Roach" (140).

The pressures on Jack Kerouac's naming procedures were diverse. Like many Americans still living, Kerouac's experience bridged two radically different eras, the Great Depression and the postwar boom, and like many children of immigrants he was reared in a foreign language but grew up into English. *The Town and the City* begins in the 1930s with an anonymous figure musing over the ethnic names on the tombstones in the Galloway cemetery (4); in *Vanity of Duluoz*, on the other hand, the narrator recalls with chagrin that his mates on board a Liberty Ship during the first year of World War II couldn't even pronounce his French surname (140). According to biographer Gerald Nicosia, "People misspelled and often deliberately mispronounced [Kerouac's] name" (21), and a common campy form of fun among his later Beat companions was to use puns to invent odd names for their friends (111), a game that may have originated with Jack and Edie (315).

Kerouac's method of spontaneous composition strove to match the mass production of the 1950s with a rapid outpouring of prose, and his dedication to the complementary confessional modes of Roman Catholicism (excmplified by the fifth century *Confessions* of St. Augustine) and French Romanticism (exemplified by the late eighteenth century *Confessions* of Jean-Jacques Rousseau), besides connecting him with the 1950s mainstream trend towards confessional poetry, further committed him to a fictional practice that placed a high value on honesty and sincerity. In *Satori in Paris*, his next-to-last novel, Kerouac insists condescendingly that…made up stories and romances about
  what would happen IF are for children and adult cretins who are

afraid to read themselves in a book just as they might be afraid to look in the mirror when they're sick or injured or hungover or insane. (10)

As both his manuscripts and his manifestos attest, Jack never intended to use character names at all in his mature writing, and his preference for verity over verisimilitude has led to some interesting dilemmas. When Kerouac submitted a manuscript of *On the Road* in which characters bore the names of their real-life models, the lawyers at Viking Press—perhaps sensitized by the passage of the Defamation Act in England in 1952—objected (Nicosia 495). John Clellon Holmes, Kerouac's friend and fellow writer, recalls, however, that the use of real names for characters in a first draft was common in their circle at that time (Gifford and Lee 157). In contemporary journalism the identity of persons named in news stories and their real life counterparts continues to form the basis of an editor's ability to determine—and to a large extent the basis for the readers' belief—that such news stories are not fictions, that is, fabrications that emanate solely or largely from the writer's imagination. The ten biographies of Kerouac published since 1973 testify to the fact that many of his readers take this journalistic approach in attempting to identify his characters with their real-life counterparts, with the effect that Kerouac's novels are perceived more as reportage than as imaginative constructs. Kerouac, of course, encouraged this view of his work by incorporating in *Book of Dreams* tables that show the equivalence of a number of character names in four of his books (5–6), suggesting that in several instances four different characters are based on the same model. In their "oral" biography of Jack, Barry Gifford and Lawrence Lee follow his lead by providing an extensive identity key to the entire body of Kerouac's work cross-referenced by both character name and actual name (322–334).

In the case of *On the Road*, Kerouac was forced both to invent new names for his characters ("pseudonyms masking pseudonyms," according to Gifford and Lee xi) and to obtain signed releases from their models relinquishing their right to sue (Nicosia 495; Gifford and Lee 207). The models, who were mostly friends and fellow writers, complied graciously, but the renaming of the characters still ran against Kerouac's grain. Having rejected the naming practice of fictional realism and being forbidden to take the purely journalistic approach, he was forced to invent a hybrid process. For the name of his hero, he transformed a phrase of his friend Allen Ginsberg, "sad paradise," into Sal Paradise, creating an optimistic Pilgrim by yoking the Italian word for savior, *salvatore*, to the ultimate goal of the Christian's life journey. He borrowed Sal's brother's name, Rocco, from *Fidelio*, the Beethoven opera Sal attends in Central City, Colorado, in the first part of the novel (52). Readers have speculated that Dean Moriarty, perhaps Kerouac's most famous character, is named for the arch-villain of Arthur Conan Doyle's detective stories, suggesting Sherlock Holmes's dramatic dependence on his nemesis, Professor Moriarty, "the Napoleon of crime." Deductive reasoning supports this speculation, since in *Visions of Cody* Kerouac transformed Neal Cassady's buddy Jim Holmes into the character Tom Watson. A more mundane explanation is that Moriarty is the first town of any size to the east of Albuquerque, New Mexico, on old Route 66.

On his travels, Jack noted the names of many insignificant places, and one of these may have suggested the name of the antagonist in *On the Road*. The apparently allegorical name of a minor character in *On the Road* reinforces this theory. The self-possessed Galatea Dunkel is anything but a statue, although she is admittedly an artist's creation like her namesake in the story of Pygmalion, and her husband's love is only strong enough to bring him back to her after a month-long escapade in New York City. But her name is also the name of a town in eastern Colorado that Kerouac may have picked up from the story of one of Cassady's adolescent escapades. And Galatea is also the title of a minor 1953 novel by James M. Cain, author of the 1934 thriller *The Postman Always Rings Twice*, and its appearance during Kerouac's lengthy revision of *On the Road* may have prompted him to expropriate the name out of envy for Cain's commercial success.

Whatever the origin of the characters' names, the police, in their reading of *On the Road*, applied a crude theory of referentiality to the alias Moriarty, heeding the rumor on the street that the character represented Cassady. Further, they assumed that Dean's fictional pot-smoking represented Neal's real pot-smoking, an interpretive assumption that eventually led to Neal Cassady's arrest, conviction, and incarceration for two years. Perhaps if Kerouac's preference had been for greater fictionalization rather than lesser, Cassady might not have lost his job, his freedom, and his wife, but the media rather than the novelist were primarily to blame for a police crackdown on beatniks in San Francisco's North Beach (Rigney and Smith 157–161). Yet it does seem odd that Jack disguised his authorial identity more carefully than the identities of his companions in *On the Road* (and in *The Dharma Bums* as well), so much so that some readers later mistook him as the model for Dean Moriarty rather than Sal Paradise (Gifford and Lee 242).

Allen Ginsberg, who was so thrilled with Kerouac's characterization of him as Leon Levinsky in *The Town and the City* that he wrote a poem in honor of that character ("Sweet Levinsky," *Poems* 19 [Kerouac may have borrowed this character name from Abraham Cahan's 1917 masterpiece, *The Rise of David Lavinsky*]), in *On the Road* becomes Carlo Marx, a rounder character than his name, a flatly allegorical representation of his mother's Communist background and his own left-wing politics, suggests. Other characters besides Paradise, Moriarty, Galatea, and Marx bear this allegorical stamp in their names as well. Justin Brierly, the well-heeled Colorado attorney who encouraged Neal Cassady to go to New York in 1946, was first called Beattie G. Davies (Gifford and Lee 205), then became Denver D. Doll in the novel, while Henri Cru, Kerouac's prep school classmate and fellow francophone—invariably called Deni Bleu in later novels—becomes Remi Boncoeur, a name Kerouac explicates for faithful followers of the Duluoz Legend in *Desolation Angels*, where the narrator translates the French words for "good heart" (275).

But some of the charactonyms in *On the Road* exemplify a third process used by Kerouac, a combination of realistic and poetic approaches, that is, the practice of using sound effects to mimic the real names of the models, a kind of onomastic onomatopoeia that Bruce Cook dubbed "Kerouacese" (29, 64). Substituting Dunkel for Hinckle, the real surname of Helen (another problematic beauty), model for Galatea, gives an indication of how this process works. Kerouac usually preserves both the consonant and vowel sounds of the original names and the original number of syllables, providing him with a simple, easy, and aesthetically satisfying process for renaming. In later novels, for example, Hinckle is transformed into Buckle. Likewise, Hal Chase, the archaeologist who introduced Cassady to Kerouac, appears as Chad King, Lucien (Carr) becomes Damion, and Bob Burford's alliterative name is transformed into Ray Rawlins, though his sister, Beverly, becomes Babe Rawlins, thanks to Kerouac's wolfish compliment in the masked shortened form of her first name. Thus, throughout the Duluoz Legend, real life names like Gary Snyder are transformed by this simple process into Japhy Ryder in *The Dharma Bums* (Cook 29) or Jarry Wagner in *Desolation Angels*. Kerouac's contemporary, Alan Harrington, called Hal Hingham in *On the Road* (165), noticed the process and returned the favor by adopting Jack's naming procedure in his retrospective 1966 novel, *The Secret Swinger,* where Kerouac appears as Jan Crehore, who "inspired America's young people with a big, traveling novel that he wrote in two months" (55).

Kerouac sometimes stretches his naming process—which only occasionally reverts to standard allegory in such charactonyms as Rheinhold Cacoethes (that is, mania—which still preserves, inverted, the initial consonant sounds of the original name) for the overbearing San Francisco man of letters Kenneth Rexroth in *The Dharma Bums*—into punning. In *Desolation Angels*, for instance, the founder and director of the San Francisco Poetry Center, Ruth Witt Diamant, is wittily transfigured into Rose Wise Lazuli, preserving the cadence of her name while elevating the liveliness of her mind and associating her last name with another precious stone in Yeats's beautiful poem about the permanence of art, "Lapis Lazuli" (Yeats 294–295). Similarly, in the same novel the character Alex Aums (that is, the sacred syllable Om) represents the great popularizer of Zen Buddhism Alan Watts.

Such punning names often provide a key to Kerouac's feelings about the real-life models as well as an index of his sense of humor. As Dan Wakefield long ago observed, Kerouactonyms are like "funny hats" the author provided for the people in his life (qtd. in Gifford & Lee 322), people he viewed proprietarily as his "millions of characters" (*Desolation Angels* 13). For instance, Kerouac made Lou Little, the Columbia football coach he blamed for ruining both his and his father's careers, into Lu Libble in *Vanity of Duluoz,* but in order to twist the knife, Duluoz also reveals that Libble's "real" name is Guido Pistola (51), an allusion to Little's disguised Italian-American heritage. On the other hand, in *Desolation Angels* Kerouac expresses his sympathy for the painter Robert LaVigne by calling him by Jack's mother's family name, Levesque, at the same time that he suggests that Robert is the reincarnation of Jack's saintly brother, Gerard (191). He pokes fun at another prep school classmate, Seymour Wyse, by calling him Lionel Smart in *Vanity of Duluoz*, while also recalling that one of their teachers had nicknamed him "Nutso" (23), and in *Satori in Paris* (96) Duluoz associates this same old friend with Seymour Glass, the troubled young man who commits suicide at the end of J. D. Salinger's "A Perfect Day for Bananafish" (Salinger 3–26).

For Gregory Corso, the young poet who in the early 1950s became the fourth member of the Beat circle, Kerouac betrays a brotherly combination of admiration, protection, and contempt. In *The Subterraneans*, the title of which is intended to suggest Dostoevsky's "Notes from Underground," the syllable count of Corso's first and last names is reversed, his Italian ethnicity is converted into Russian, and his slight speech impediment is put on display in the name for his character, Yuri Gligoric (the last name representing a slurred version of Gregory, as well as being the name of a real-life 1950s Russian chess champion). In later novels Kerouac, now preserving the actual rhythm of the original name, settled on Raphael Urso for Corso. In a self-conscious passage in *Desolation Angels*, in fact, he compares this character name with the original and connects it etymologically with his later "uniform" name for Neal Cassady, Cody Pomeray, which combines the surname of the famous Western hero, Buffalo Bill, with that of a sexologist Kerouac met in the late 1940s (Sandison 88). "Urso and Pomeray," the narrator explains, "both their names mean something that may have once been Casa D'Oro, which would make it no coarser than Corso" (139). Here, of course, Kerouac is both punning on the names of his characters and playfully revealing their true identities (Casa D'=Cassady) as he also announces his growing interest in the derivation of the names.

As I have already suggested, this contradictory tendency to conceal and reveal the identity of his characters also plays a regular role in Kerouac's naming process. For example, in a passage in *The Dharma Bums* in which Ray Smith, the Kerouac character, returns to meet Japhy, the Gary Snyder character, Ray says, "I had a dollar left and Gary was waiting for me at the shack" (161). In a 1982 note, the British Kerouac critic Chris Challis questioned whether this substitution of the model's real name was an oversight on the part of author or proofreader (Item 13), and though Challis doubted that the author's intention could ever be established, I like to think it was Kerouac's way of playing a little prank on Viking Penguin in order to preserve the character's true identity for posterity in spite of the publisher's attorneys (see Gifford and Lee 243, where Kerouac's annoyance at the editing of *The Dharma Bums* is described).

The authorial intention is much clearer in the case of two fellows who share the first name Bill, which becomes Bull in Kerouacese. Bull Gaines, Jack's name for William Maynard Garver, a notorious New York coat thief who emigrated to Mexico City in the early 1950s, is unmasked in *Desolation Angels* when Gaines's Spanish-speaking landlady greets him as "'Senor Garv-ha'" (226). At the end of the novel, when Duluoz returns to Mexico City, he learns of the character's and the actual man's death. While one report says, "'Senor Gaines se murio,'" the neighborhood storekeeper tells Jack, "'Senor Gahr-va se murio" (365).

Kerouac follows the same practice in revealing the identity of his close friend and fellow novelist William S. Burroughs, who is called Bull Hubbard in the same novel, a last name borrowed from "J. Arthur Rank's production of...*Four Feathers* in which there is a fellow called Hubbard in the story" (*Vanity of Dolouz* 177). (It is worth noting that Kerouac saw this British film in 1944 with his friend Lucien Carr, who had just committed murder.) At any rate, when they walk together through the streets of Tangiers in *Desolation Angels*, Jack observes, "Everybody seems to know him. Boys yell 'Hi!' 'Boorows!' 'Hey!'" (307). No doubt the association of Burroughs's name with the word *burro* is also intended as a friendly dig at his mentor.

The revelation of Burroughs's identity in *On the Road* is more convoluted. Apparently, his stepdaughter, Julie, "called Bill 'Bull', because she could not pronounce the name" (Huncke 90), and Kerouac simply appropriated her baby-talk to name his character. For the surname of the character Old Bull Lee, Kerouac borrows the pseudonym Burroughs employed to disguise himself in his self-incriminating first novel, *Junkie*, which title appeared over the name William Lee. In his book-length poem *Mexico City Blues*, where Kerouac felt no pressure to fictionalize the names, the speaker of the "5th Chorus" simply trumpets the news: "William Burroughs / Is William Lee" (5). If Burroughs had not already been on the run from the law, he might have suffered from the same kind of police interpretation as Neal Cassady, thanks to his friend's authorial insistence on honesty.

Frequently in his literary portraiture Kerouac combines character names with physical descriptions of the models as another way of revealing the identities of the characters to those in the know. His well-known description of the epoch-making Six Gallery (or Gallery Six, as it is called in *The Dharma Bums*) reading in San Francisco in October 1955 provides a perfect example:

> The other poets were either hornrimmed intellectual hepcats with wild black hair like Alvah Goldbook, or delicate pale handsome poets like Ike O'Shay (in a suit), or out-of-this-world genteel-looking Renaissance Italians like Francis Da Pavia (who looks like a young priest), or bow-tied wild-haired old anarchist fuds like Rheinhold Cacoethes, or big fat bespectacled quiet booboos like Warren Coughlin. (*The Dharma Bums* 12)

Such concise description serves both the purpose of artistic economy and as an insider's key to the identities of, respectively, Allen Ginsberg, Michael McClure, Philip Lamantia, Kenneth Rexroth, and Philip Whalen (who is also described somewhat too objectively as "a hundred eighty pounds of poet meat" [11]).

In Book One of *Desolation Angels*, a sequel to the last scene in *The Dharma Bums*, Kerouac paints rather unflattering portraits of James Merrill and Randall Jarrell, where Merrill becomes Merrill Randall, a name probably designed to suggest that he is indistinguishable from the other poet, and Jarrell becomes Varnum Random, combining the name of a street in Lowell on which Kerouac's family once lived with a word obviously intended to disparage Jarrell's similarity to other conventional poets of his generation. Kerouac reserves the unrestrained praise of positive portraiture in *Desolation Angels* for Robert Duncan, who is called by Chaucer's first name combined with an imitatively Scottish given name, Geoffrey Donald. Here, Donald, age 32, looks "plump, fair-faced, sad-eyed, elegant" (144), and Duluoz explains that the poet is "an elegant sadweary type who's been to Europe, to Ischia and Capri and such, known the rich elegant writers and types, and had just spoken for me to a New York publisher so I am surprised (first time I meet him)" (149, parentheses in original). Much of this language, especially the conspicious repetition of the word *elegant*, seems coded to reveal Duncan's sexual orientation, in addition to underscoring his ethnicity (a habit Kerouac carried with him from the earliest days in Lowell) and disclosing his identity. Fortunately, Duncan had come out more than ten years earlier.

As he grew into middle age Kerouac developed an interest in genealogy that often manifests itself as an obsession with the origin of his surname, as though by studying his family history he could make the broad vowels and sharp consonants of their name mean something besides itself. In *Satori in Paris* he gives Kerouac the meaning "House in the field" (72), relating it to the word *bivouac*, but just a few years later in *Vanity of Duluoz*, he revises its meaning to "Language of the House" (94). Because his own name had always struck anglophone ears as strange, his preoccupation with it signifies more than a desire to trace his roots. Kerouac's name presented difficult questions about his identity, and nothing is more revealing of his fictional naming process than the names he substitutes for Kerouac throughout the Duluoz Legend.

As I have already mentioned, Jack spoke mostly French until he began school, so his early years resounded with nicknames unfamiliar to English speakers. His parents called him Ti Jean, short for *petit* Jean, or sometimes Ti Pousse, little thumb, because he was so plump. In the English-speaking world his given name was anglicized to John Louis, for practical reasons he explained much later in *Satori in Paris*:

"...you can't go around America and join the Merchant Marine and be called 'Jean'" (95). In *Dr. Sax* the young narrator's heroic alter ego is called Jack Lewis, eliminating the French spelling of the middle name (in *Maggie Cassidy* the protagonist's rival in a track meet bears an African American equivalent, John Henry Lewis). Later in his childhood Ti Jean was anglicized to the diminutive Jacky, and in adolescence his pals prophetically nicknamed him Zagg, after one of the town drunks in Lowell (*Vanity of Duluoz* 45), and Memory Babe, because of his prodigious recall. As he grew older he became known to most people as Jack, but *The Town and the City* bore the name John Kerouac on its title page, apropos of the serious-looking, sharply dressed, dark young man pictured on the back of the dust jacket. Not until he enrolled in creative writing classes in the late 1940s at the New School for Social Research (called "the Modern School of Cultural Research" in this first published novel [*The Town and the City* 459]) did he begin to sign his literary work as he had bylined his stories for the *Horace Mann Record* in 1939—Jack Kerouac (Hunt 106).

His first choice for a name to represent himself as a character in his own fiction is Peter George Martin, after the apostle who denied Christ and the father of his family saga in *The Town and the City* (in *Book of Dreams*, by the way, Jack calls the Martins—an actual French family name in Lowell—the "Kerouacs of my soul" [17]). Next, in *On the Road* he substituted Italian for French ancestry in the name of Sal Paradise, and later he resorted to a self-consciously allegorical French Leo Percepied, combining his father's real given name with the French equivalent of Oedipus in *The Subterraneans*.

In 1951 or 1952, during the revision of *On the Road* but before writing *The Subterraneans*, Kerouac dredged up a character name for himself he had used first in 1941—Duluoz (though his first name at that time was Bob)—which he installed in his most experimental novel, *Visions of Cody*. In a letter to Neal Cassady he associated his fictional name for himself with the young protagonist in James Joyce's *A Portrait of the Artist as a Young Man*, Stephen Daedalus, himself named for the mythical Greek artificer (Charters 296). Because of a misunderstanding created by Kerouac's first biographer in her reading of

Vanity of Duluoz, where other characters sometimes call the hero Dulouse, this name was assumed to be self-deprecating. In fact, as Kerouac reveals in *Satori in Paris*, it was intended to represent his Breton heritage (101), though it also derives from Daoulas, a Greek family name still listed in the Lowell phone book.

Though Kerouac may have invented it much earlier, the name Duluoz made its first public appearance alongside a super-realistic tape transcription in *Visions of Cody*, where readers also find Jackie Duluoz's sixth-grade composition about Roger Buttock, a descendent of the Buttock Bank Indians (250), as well as a news story about a forger named Jack L. Duluoz from Compton, California (254). Readers likewise encounter here satirical names such as Ernest Hummingbird and Clyde Cockmaster and find that Joan Crawford on the set of the 1952 film *Sudden Fear* has been grotesquely rechristened Joan Rawshanks (275). In *Dr. Sax* (composed mostly in 1952) eleven-year-old Jackie Duluoz joins the company of some very bizarre characters, such as Count Condu (French for one who is led or driven); Amadeus Baroque (which combines Mozart's middle name with his musical period); Epzebiah Phloggett—alias Smogette Phloggett—a combination, perhaps, of Hepzebiah Pyncheon, the main character in Nathaniel Hawthorne's *House of Seven Gables*, and Phineas Fogg, the hero of Jules Verne's *Around the World in Eighty Days*; a priest named La Poule du Puis (French for "the hen of then"); Orabus Flabus, whose name suggests that of Orville Faubus, the notorious Arkansas governor and anti-civil rights leader of the period; and a cat with the whimsical name of Pondu Pokie. Dr. Sax himself, whose name is that of Kerouac's favorite jazz instrument and who bears a striking resemblance to the comic book hero The Shadow, is disparagingly called "Flaxy Sax with his big Nax" by one of his enemies in the novel (224) and identified by the narrator as a "disease of the night" called Visagus Nightsoil (21), suggesting the unflattering reflection of a face in a slop-jar. After the experiment of *Visions of Cody,* the compostion of Kerouac's novel of puberty swung to the opposite pole from realism, unleashing a plethora of imaginative names that add an unusual note of childlike humor to the gothic atmosphere of *Dr. Sax*.

Even after settling on Duluoz as a standard name for his own fictional character, however, Kerouac continued to invent other names to simultaneously represent and disguise himself. As I already noted, he transformed himself into a French Oedipus for *The Subterraneans,* an Italian Nick Carraway for *On the Road*, and a perfectly anglicized American hobo, Ray Smith, for *The Dharma Bums*, but even these narrators have the freedom to invent new masks for their creator. In *The Subterraneans,* where Paradise Alley in Greenwich Village is transmuted into San Francisco's Heavenly Lane, Leo gives himself the unbelievable alias Finn MacPossipy (65), fusing the legendary Irish hero Finn MacCool with a Pogo-like cartoon animal. One of Sal's traveling companions in *On the Road* nicknames him Blackie (32), like a typical outlaw, probably because of his dark hair, while Carlo Marx tags Dean with the much more suggestive title "Oedipus Eddie" (48). The good-hearted Remi threatens to start calling Sal "Dostioffski" (i.e., dusty-off-ski, purposely mispronouncing the name of one of Kerouac's biggest literary idols) if he doesn't liven up (69), and with his old college writing buddy Roland Major, Sal role-plays the character Sam in an imaginary Hemingway story (78). A young African American woman mistakes Sal for an anonymous "Joe" (181), while Dean is transformed by Sal's imagination into Melville's Ahab (236), Rabelais' Gargantua (259), and America's F.D.R. (283). Finally, when Stan Shepard's ailing granddaddy mistakes Sal for Dean (266), the companions' identities become interchangeable. In *The Dharma Bums* Ray Smith canonizes himself as the Catholic St. Raymond of the Dogs (145) and the Buddhist Bhikku Blank Rat ((146), while his buddy the Buddhist janitor Bud Diefendorf (based on real-life friend Claude Dahlenberg [Gifford & Lee 325]) becomes "the no-name Bhikku" (176). In his fire-lookout cabin at the end of the novel Ray is terrified by the real names of the surrounding north Cascades peaks: Mount Terror, Mount Fury, Mount Despair, and his own Desolation Peak.

Duluoz and his variants seem to have a hundred identities: in *Desolation Angels* alone he is a sexual outlaw with the improbable name of Erdaway Moliere (12), "Old Navajoa Jacko the Yaqui Walkin Champeen and Saint of the Self-Forgotten Night" (93), the Chihuahua Kid (96),

Priam (203), and finally "Who-Are-You, Ass?" (273), by which the author ironically reveals his identity with the narrator. Like the character Mal Damlette, who represents Kerouac's seaman buddy Al Sublette in *Desolation Angels* (139), Memory Babe could have just as easily been nicknamed "the Namer." Not content to rename himself once, Kerouac seems determined to rename even the characters he has invented to impersonate him, as though by distancing himself further and further from his created selves he hoped finally to escape—or at least locate—his own identity.

Two

Does an awareness of Kerouac's naming procedure help readers to understand his writing, beyond providing a literary puzzle for the biographically inclined? Obviously, I think it does, in two ways. The first way involves the practical matter of exegesis; the second way is more writerly, if ultimately metaphysical, in its import.

An example of the first way in which sensitivity to the names helps the reader evaluate the text can be found in a crucial passage in Kerouac's novel of alcoholic dementia, *Big Sur*, published in 1961. The events of this novel lie on the downhill side of the Duluoz Legend, after Kerouac has already come to realize that his life is not going to turn out the way he had hoped. He knows now that he is incapable of starting his own family, but he persists bravely in the attempt in the face of his own despair. His attempt takes the shape of a preposterous relationship with a single mother whom he barely knows, a woman called Billie in the novel, modeled on Jackie Gibson, a lover Neal Cassady had passed along to his friend. In the midst of the chaos of Duluoz's third and final visit to an oceanside cabin, as their brief affair begins to disintegrate, Billie threatens to commit suicide. In a visionary moment Duluoz perceives over her forlorn figure in the surf the words "SAINT CAROLYN BY THE SEA" (182).

The full purport of this climactic scene is lost on readers who are unaware of the intricacies of Kerouac's fictional names. Carolyn is the real name of Neal Cassady's wife, and in her memoir, *Off the Road*, she recounts at length an earlier three-way love affair between Neal, Jack, and herself. Duluoz's attempt to bond with Billie in *Big Sur* had stimulated Kerouac's growing awareness that his failure in love was self-determined, the result of his oedipal relationship with his mother, which compelled him throughout his life to choose for lovers women attached to brother-figures. His love for Carolyn Cassady had come to represent the epitome of his predicament. His vision of Jackie and the failure entailed by his relationship with her prompted him both to associate her with Carolyn and to reveal Carolyn's identity, but since her character in *Big Sur* is called Evelyn Pomeray, only the reader with biographical knowledge and a feel for the tricks of Kerouac's name game will appreciate the full effect of Duluoz's confession.

The second advantage of understanding Kerouactonyms is more theoretical in that it bears on both the author's psychology and the form of his work. When the first book-length studies of Kerouac began to be written, critics were quick to perceive that Jack's method of characterization served to help him display, analyze, and sometimes transcend conflicts in his own personality. Warren French, for example, found that "his linguistic background is almost certainly responsible for a deep split in Kerouac's personality which persisted throughout his early years and which suggests the reason for his dividing himself into the complementary characters of Peter and Francis Martin in *The Town and the City*" (4). John Tytell, one of the earliest and most perceptive critics of Beat literature, detected a similar conflict in Kerouac's letters of the mid-1950s: "That Kerouac was beginning to wonder about his own identity is suggested by the way he kept changing his name as he signed letters, from Jack, to Jean, to Jean-Louis, to Jack-off or Jockolio" (73). We know now that Kerouac had a much more practical—if less admirable—reason for using these pseudonyms: he was trying to prevent his estranged second wife from tracking him down. In one letter from Mexico, ironically addressed to Stella Sampas, the woman who became his third wife more than ten years later, Kerouac even attempted to disguise himself by adopting his mother's family name as he signed himself "Sr. Jean Levesque" (*Letters* 389).

Nevertheless, critics like French and Tytell were on the right track. Tim Hunt, who analyzed the development of Kerouac's writing practice in the composition of the various versions of *On the Road*, spotted the contradiction between Kerouac's later fidelity to actual names and his original adherence to traditional realistic fiction. In spite of the author's insistence that his first published novel is a product of standard fictional processes, Hunt says, "The book is in many ways Kerouac's most directly autobiographical" (78). This opinion is seconded by Barry Gifford and Lawrence Lee in *Jack's Book*:

> *The Town and the City* is a fiction, with characters and incidents more imaginary than those of any other Kerouac novel, even the fantastical *Doctor Sax*. At the same time it appears to reveal more than any of the others about Jack's attitudes toward his family and himself as a very young man. (66)

Recognition of the autobiographical content of *The Town and the City* results in part from Kerouac's own account to his friend, the poet Allen Ginsberg, that as he composed it "he was splitting his mind into discrete parts and embodying each part in a different person" (Nicosia 303), and in part from a self-contradictory statement he made in a letter to the Lowell *Sun* in announcing the forthcoming publication of the novel: "It's not strictly autobiographical, since I used various friends and girl-friends, and my own parents, to form a large family, the Martin family..." (17 Dec. 1949 letter to Charles Sampas, qtd. in Jarvis 211). After the publication of the novel in 1950, he even admitted to a fan that he was both Peter and Francis and Joe, the oldest brothers in the fictional Martin family (14 January 1950 letter to Ellen Lucy, cited by French 25).

In his dissertation on the masculinist qualities of Kerouac's writing Steve Davenport argues that this split of Kerouac's personality into three characters also represents a redistribution of the internal conflicts of George Martin, the fictional father in the novel, a split that "allows all of the father's conflicting desires to be played out safely in the next generation of males" (161). Further, French finds a therapeutic value in Kerouac's formal multiplication of his own character: "By dividing the portrayal of himself between the two brothers, Kerouac was able to give the third-person narrator a distance from the action that made possible an equilibrium in the treatment of the conflicting parts of his own personality" (28). French proceeds to argue that Kerouac's subsequent novels, the ones for which he is best known, "which are dominated by a single autobiographically based figure" (28), depend for their effects on the dominance of one of the conflicting elements of Kerouac's personality at the time of composition, suggesting that in abandoning the traditional mode of realistic fiction Kerouac had also abandoned a valuable tool of psychic stability. A more recent critic has noted, however, that Peter Martin provided the prototype for Jack

Duluoz, Ray Smith, and Sal Paradise, while also recognizing that these later characters are all modeled on Kerouac himself (Foster 35). French himself observed that Sal is "a split character" who combines the personalities of Peter and Francis Martin in "a single figure who moves back and forth between two quite different lives" (37).

Such critical commentary is consistent in recognizing that a conflict in Kerouac's personality is being played out in his creation of characters, and that his shift from masking his autobiography in traditional realism to revealing it more explicitly in his later journalistic mode marks both a formal and a psychological transition in his career. Tim Hunt, the critic with the most profound insight into this transition, explains its aesthetic significance in this way: "One can only know another self imaginatively, and if the imagination is not seen as real and able to contain the conflicts of life, then one cannot know another self and may not be real oneself" (249). In other words, because of his Romantic esteem for the power of imaginative transformation, the process of characterization led Kerouac to a metaphysical impasse analogous to Freud's account of the encounter between the demands of the infant's libido and the inflexibility of the external world.

In his spontaneous prose Kerouac sought to reconcile the selves that he imagined with the selves that he encountered by blurring the boundary between fiction and fact. His discovery of his sketching method as a "vertical" complement to his rapid "horizontal" narration brought him face to face with a "dialectic in a more comprehensive form as the unresolvable opposition between the imagination as authority and the world as authority, between the enacting of self as an individual free of society and the possession of identity within and from society" (Hunt 187–188). According to Hunt, the tape transcript section of *Visions of Cody*, the experimental novel that followed from the intense and repeated revisions of *On The Road,* portrays Dulouz's discovery that self is an activity rather than an object (223), a discovery that leads to self-consciousness about both the psychic and aesthetic value of self-characterization. As Hunt further explains, " Duluoz is the side that emerges from construction, an identity that suggests Kerouac's sense of how the activity of the transcending imagination appears to society" (189–190). As a result, Hunt believes, the narrator of *Visions of Cody* "is actually more real than the Kerouac behind it, and the understanding of the Kerouac of the text transcends that of the Kerouac outside it" (190).

The implication of the superiority of the fictional reality of a character is that readers may also be led to see the process of characterization as an index of their own social and physical interactions and derive from their awareness of the complexity of the process a sense not only of the fictional qualities of identity but also of the imaginative activity involved in creating and maintaining their own personalities. For Kerouac (and potentially for his readers) the formal activity of characterization represents the psychological activity that leads to a fundamental metaphysical question: What is a self? His immediate artistic answer to this question, as he began to reach back into his early life for material for his next novels, *Dr. Sax* and *Maggie Cassidy,* was that "he must adapt himself to projecting a series of selves, each doomed to destruction in the experience of the adult and each recreated and located in the past by a child" (Hunt 250). The effect of Kerouac's repeated "process of psychic transformation," as Gregory Stephenson has called the development of the Beat hero (178), resembles nothing so much as a rite of passage in which an adolescent is ritualistically introduced into adulthood, replacing the immature self with a new, mature self. Yet as Hunt suggests, Kerouac seems to have reversed the chronology of this process, invoking the Romantic view of childhood in which the true personality is obscured or even obliterated by maturity.

Just after the composition of *The Subterraneans,* a sequel to *Maggie Cassidy* using the current events of his life rather than the past, Kerouac made the biggest discovery of his adulthood when he began an intense study of Buddhism. This discovery takes on a new significance in light of Tim Hunt's description of Kerouac's struggle to understand the nature of self and its relation to fictional characterization. One of the first books that came to Kerouac's hand was *A Buddhist Bible*, edited by Dwight Goddard and republished in 1952. As Goddard explains in his introduction, the various texts he has collected are united thematically by the Hindu principle of anatta, the quest to transcent the ego for the sake of enlightenment. Just two years after engaging in the profound struggle to understand the nature of his own personality by means of the process of fictional characterization, Kerouac read these words of the Buddha: "Call me not after my private name, for it is a rude and careless way of addressing one who has become an *Arhat*...But it is not courteous for others to call one who looks equally with a kind heart upon all loving beings by his familiar name" (Goddard 10).

Suddenly, the novelist found that his intuitive fictional naming process had a spiritual sanction and objective. His role as a follower of such personalities as Neal Cassady began to change, paving the way for his 1955 meeting with Gary Snyder, whose fictional version in *The Dharma Bums,* Japhy Ryder, became a spiritual counterbalance against the demonic materialism of Dean Moriarty. "Buddhism," as John Tydell has pointed out, "helped Kerouac transcend his own artistic ego, the supreme sense of self he had admired in men like Cassady" (76). The names in Kerouac's next three novels, *Visions of Gerard, Tristessa,* and *The Dharma Bums* constitute not only a part of his devotional practice of Buddhism through writing but also a part of his own attempts to achieve anatta for himself. While his attraction to writing undoubtedly resulted in part from his shyness—for like theater and even sports to some extent, writing is the introvert's way of being an extrovert—his attraction to Buddhism gave metaphysical significance to his instinctive desire to suppress his ego. As Joyce Johnson, his girlfriend at the time of the publication of *On The Road* in 1957, put it, Kerouac still believed that "through your book you could become known without giving yourself away" (Johnson 183). Both his personal reticence and his spiritual practice were shattered by the media's journalistic emphasis on the facts behind his fictions, revealing for the sake of news value the "true identity" of his characters despite his publisher's precautions. While such unmasking would appear to satisfy Kerouac's desire for total honesty, on some deeper level it interfered with his private attempt to conduct a more subtle analysis of human identity.

Kerouac's precipitous physical and psychological decline in the early 1960s testifies to his naivete about celebrity. All his spiritual and artistic (not to mention psychological and metaphysical) investment in escaping from his own ego was nullified in one fell swoop by a media blitz that succeeded only in creating caricatures of personality called beatniks and commodified the fluid activity of Kerouac's personality by crowning him their king. Still, the resilience of his "name game" (Nicosia 347) pays tribute to Kerouac's struggles in the early 1950s and the persistence of the insights he won then. Despite his alcoholism and apparent cynicism, he continued to write, and after reaching his nadir in 1965 in the last chronological installment of the Duluoz Legend, *Satori in Paris*, he returned in his last novel, *Vanity of Duluoz*, not to his ideal of using the real names of the models of his fictional creations but to his "pantheon of uniform names" in his revision of the overly fictionalized *The Town and the City*.

There is a sense in this reversion that character names convert the heterogeneous population of Kerouac's life into a fictional family, as Robert Creeley has called it (*Good Blonde & Others* xi), despite his avowed intention to forego the fictionalization of their actions, making them an important formal principle of the episodic, autobiographical Duluoz Legend. If in all his novels, as John Tytell observed, "Kerouac is usually hard on his persona, almost always making him a projection of a failure he felt in his own life" (197), this self-censure was a product of the profound introspection prerequisite to literature, and the name Duluoz—whether it means "the louse" or something more positive—exposes a serious flaw in Robert Hipkiss's assertion that "we are seldom allowed to smile at Kerouac's heroes" (104). The names in Kerouac's books represent a hard-won, philosophical lightheartedness about personality, a feature of human existence that Jack Kerouac recognized has been endowed by American culture with far too much gravity, stability, and reality.

Finally, as Kerouactonyms reveal, far from being holy, personality, though perhaps necessary, is basically silly. And ultimately, to understand Kerouac's naming process is to understand his desire—and perhaps the desire of every Romantic writer—to transcend words by means of words, to escape the limits of self by creating other, fictional selves, while at the same time recognizing that characterization itself is both a mode and an instrument to sublimate and refine our sense of the meaning of identity.

Three

In the fall of 1994 I chanced upon an unusual obituary in the St. Louis *Post-Dispatch*. In the brief article Beverly Burford DeBerard is identified as the original of Babe Rawlins in *On the Road* (30 September 1994:10D). How odd, I thought, that a woman who had apparently accomplished much in her own right should be remembered in the media as a character in a Kerouac novel. This simple reference demonstrates how thoroughly the once-maligned Beat legend has been assimilated into mainstream society, and that assimilation in turn testifies to the ongoing power of legend in the age of science and information.

In a Buddhist elegy in which Kerouac is addressed as "noble Poet," Allen Ginsberg once asked by way of title, "What Died?" (*Poems* 689). Ginsberg believed that Kerouac, as a pop culture icon and a literary legend, lives both because he was idolized and because he is read. Beverly Burford, on the other hand, lives only for her friends and family because she was loved, but she also lives for a larger public because she was renamed by her old friend Jack Kerouac. Mrs. DeBerard's obituary mimics the conflation of the death of character and model Bill Garver suffers at the end of *Desolation Angels*, and so when she died, as was the case with Garver, part of her continued to live, thanks to Jack Kerouac. While her soul has gone on its private journey into the afterlife, the name Babe Rawlins arises again whenever an energetic reader picks up one of the tens of thousands of copies of *On the Road* still being printed over forty years after it was first published.

Is this merely a postmodern permutation of necrophilia, as Kerouac himself suspected of the public reaction to James Dean's death in 1955 (*Desolation Angels* 192)? Or does every autobiographical novelist practice a kind of necromancy? Surely we foster legends, however limited they may be, at least in part to give ourselves a palpable sense of impalpable immortality. What died? Perhaps the perishable part, but not the character. And perhaps the character's name has helped preserve the essence of the living woman for a larger posterity.

By synchronicity, the week I finished writing this essay, the following death notice appeared in the Sunday *Seattle Times*:

> Anton Rosenberg, 71, a sometime artist and occasional musician who embodied the Greenwich Village hipster ideal of the 1950s and is best known as the model for the character Julian Alexander in Jack Kerouac's novel *The Subterraneans*, Feb. 14.

It has apparently now become standard policy to identify Kerouac's acquaintances as models for his fictional characters, granting them journalistic as well as novelistic immortality. In an age dominated by the mass media, no greater evidence of his influence on our culture could be found than this subtle spiritual wedge he has driven into the materialistic monolith of American individuality.

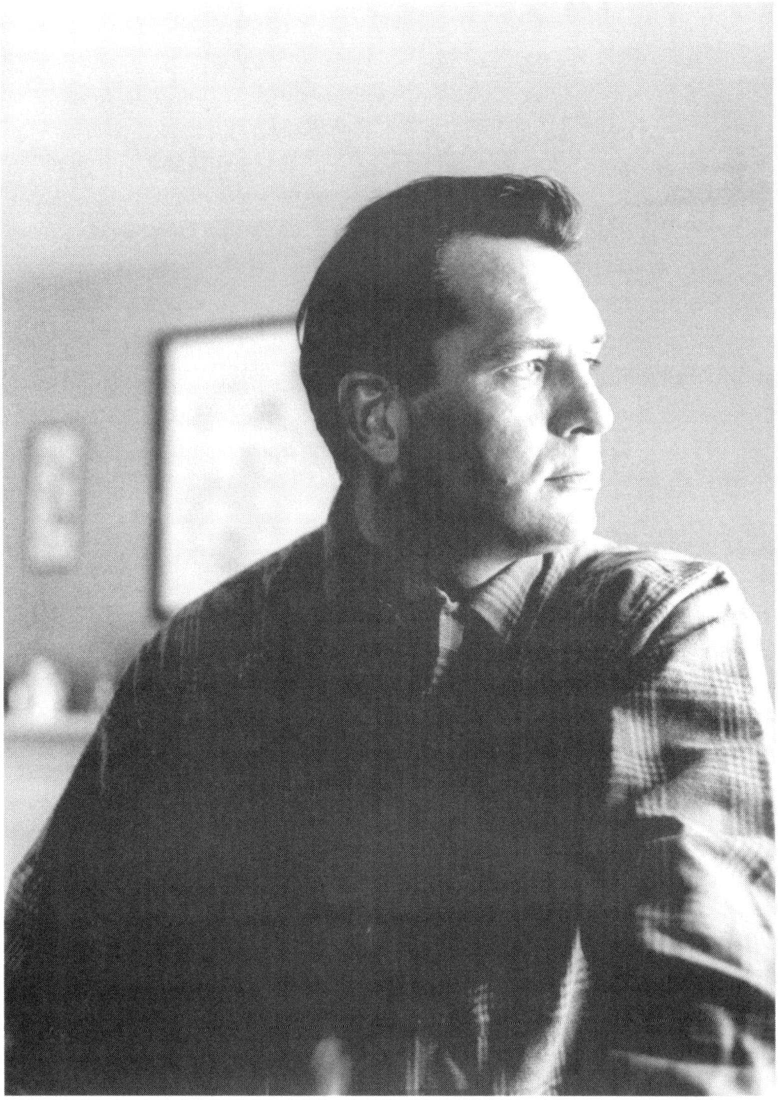

Kerouac in Seattle

If you are from the Northwest or you were living in the area when you read Jack Kerouac's classic postwar adventure novel, *On the Road*, you may have noticed that late in the novel Dean Moriarty writes to his "old man in jail in Seattle" (252), a suggestion that the infamous Neal Cassady's father once lived here. Maybe you ate in Jack's Restaurant in Ballard, where there was a parking space reserved for "Mr. Kerouac." Or perhaps you have seen Vincent Balestri's excellent one-man show, *Kerouac*, which played at the Velvet Elvis in Pioneer Square from 1994 through 1998, the latest in a series of local theater productions based on Jack's life and works. You have undoubtedly heard rumors of the George Washington-slept-here variety that Kerouac used to hole up in the Jell-O-Mold building or drink at the Blue Moon tavern, indications of his legendary presence in the city. Perhaps you have even been fortunate enough to hear jazz poet and painter Ted Joans or to meet the Beat artist Robert LaVigne, both of whom knew Kerouac and now live in Seattle.

Those who have read more of Kerouac's twenty published books, particularly *The Dharma Bums, Desolation Angels, Lonesome Traveler,* and *Book of Blues*, the four in which he discusses the Northwest at length, are aware that Jack spent about two months in the summer of 1956 as a fire lookout on Desolation Peak on the east side of Ross Lake in the North Cascades. It has now become *de rigeur* for the more physically fit Kerouac fanatic to make a pilgrimage to the many-windowed cabin in which the author spent sixty-three days confronting his demons. In the summer of 1996, the local paper featured an article by a recent Desolation fire-watcher about her experience spending a summer in the cabin (Maureen O'Neill, "Keeping Company with Kerouac," *Seattle Times*, 9 June 1996: *Pacific* sec. 20), and in April 1998 Bravo aired a profile of Kerouac featuring Boston photographer John Suiter, who argues there and in a March/April 1998 article in *Sierra* magazine that Jack's experience on Desolation Peak was a watershed in his life, the turning point into despair that embittered the fame that followed the publication of *On the Road* in September 1957.

As far as I can tell from his own writing, Jack Kerouac spent only two nights in Seattle, one June 20, 1956, on his way up to report at the Marblemount station of the U.S. Forest Service, and the other Wednesday, September 12, on his way back down to San Francisco and "south in the direction of my intended loving arms of senoritas" (*Desolation Angels* 7). By his own account, he slept both times in the old Stevens Hotel at the northeast corner of Marion and First Avenue, which was torn down in the early 1970s to make way for the new Federal Building.

Kerouac was encouraged to apply for the fire lookout job by two writers who had grown up in the Northwest, Philip Whalen and Gary Snyder, whom Jack met in San Francisco in the fall of 1955. Both Whalen, who went to high school in The Dalles, and Snyder, whose parents owned a small farm south of Seattle, had worked for the Forest Service in previous summers. The two met while attending Reed College in Portland and subsequently migrated south along with their roommate Lew Welch to become important figures in the San Francisco Renaissance. Kerouac's letters to Whalen and Snyder during the winter of 1955-56 document both his eager anticipation of his wilderness experience and the facts of his journey west.

On February 7, 1956, less than a month after he finished the composition of *Visions of Gerard*, his paean to his dead older brother, Kerouac wrote to Whalen from his sister's home in Rocky Mount, North Carolina, to say that he had just received "an offer to be the Lookout on Desolation Peak in Mt. Baker National Forest" and to thank him for his recommendation (*Letters* 547). Apparently, Whalen had applied for a lookout job himself, and Kerouac looked forward to hitchhiking up the coast with his new buddy. On March 8, Jack wrote to Snyder, who had sent him his drawing of the peak just to the north of Desolation,

Mount Hozomeen, which Kerouac felt had "a jagged sharp menacing look" (*Letters* 567), prophetic of Hozomeen's role in Kerouac's soul-searching of the coming summer. The day before he left North Carolina, Jack wrote to Carolyn Cassady that he felt this was "a crucial moment but a JOYOUS moment" in his life (*Letters* 572).

Instead of making a bee-line to the Bay Area, where he was supposed to meet editor Malcolm Cowley to discuss the revision of *On the Road*, Jack took the long way to the West Coast by way of El Paso, eventually joining Snyder in a small cabin in Mill Valley, just across the Golden Gate Bridge from San Francisco, and missing Cowley in the process. The two men spent several weeks discussing Buddhism, partying, and hiking the mountain trails of Marin County. One fine California spring night Kerouac carefully composed his imitation sutra, *The Scripture of the Golden Eternity*, and a few weeks later, imitating James Joyce, dashed off a spontaneous, stream-of-consciousness creation story called *Old Angel Midnight*. Snyder, whose grandfather had been a Wobbly organizer, further indoctrinated Kerouac in the history and lore of the Northwest and commemorated his friend's presence in the poem "Migration of Birds," which bears the date April 1956 (subsequently published in *Rip-Rap*). After Gary left for Japan in May, Jack wrote him to say that he had been "called to show up on June 25" at Marblemount ranger station in the North Cascades and that he was resolved to spend his time on the mountaintop drug-free (*Letters* 582). Before he left, however, Kerouac also met the poet Robert Creeley and became implicated in Creeley's affair with the wife of Kenneth Rexroth, which unfairly earned Jack a powerful literary enemy.

On June 18, 1956, Kerouac began hitchhiking north on the breathtaking coast highway, arriving in Crescent City, California, at dawn the next day after an all-night ride. Jack spent his second night on the road in his sleeping bag on the outskirts of Eugene, Oregon, and in the morning he caught his first sight of the Cascades. In *The Dharma Bums* he describes the third day of his trip with a wonderful economy of detail:

> In downtown Portland I took the twenty-five-cent bus to Vancouver Washington, ate a Coney Island hamburger there, then out on the road, 99, where a sweet young mustached one-kidney Bodhisattva

> Okie picked me up and said "I'm so proud I picked you up, someone to talk to," and everywhere we stopped for coffee he played the pinball machines with dead seriousness and also he picked up all hitchhikers on the road, first a big drawling Okie from Alabama then a crazy sailor from Montana who was full of crazed intelligent talk and we balled right up to Olympia Washington at eighty m.p.h. then up Olympic Peninsula on curvy woodsroads to the Naval Base at Bremerton Washington where a fifty-cent ferry ride was all that separated me from Seattle! (*The Dharma Bums* 220)

His entry into the city by ferry at dusk provides an occasion for some classic Kerouac prose. Gary Snyder, by the way, appears in the novel in the guise of Japhy Ryder:

> …I went topdeck as the ferry pulled out in a cold drizzle to dig and enjoy Puget Sound. It was one hour sailing to the Port of Seattle and I found a half-pint of vodka stuck in the deck rail concealed under a *Time* magazine and just casually drank it and opened my rucksack and took out my warm sweater to go under my rain jacket and paced up and down all alone on the cold fog-swept deck feeling wild and lyrical. And suddenly I saw that the Northwest was a great deal more than the little vision I had of it of Japhy in my mind. It was miles and miles of unbelievable mountains grooking on all horizons in the wild broken clouds, Mount Olympus and Mount Baker, a giant orange sash in the gloom over the Pacific-ward skies that led I knew toward the Hokkaido Siberian desolations of the world. I huddled against the bridgehouse hearing the Mark Twain talk of the skipper and the wheelman inside. In the deepened dusk fog ahead the big red neons saying: PORT OF SEATTLE. And suddenly everything Japhy had ever told me about Seattle began to seep into me like cold rain, I could feel it and see it now, and not just think it. It was exactly like he'd said: wet, immense, timbered, mountainous, cold, exhilarating, challenging. The ferry nosed in at the pier on Alaskan Way and immediately I saw the totem poles in old stores and the ancient 1880-style switch goat with sleepy firemen chug chugging up and down the waterfront spur like a scene from my own dreams, the old Casey Jones locomotive of America, the only one I ever saw that old outside of Western movies, but actually working and hauling boxcars in the smoky gloom of the magic city.

Here I must confront the local legend that Kerouac slept in the Jell-O-Mold building, located on Western Avenue at Bell Street, when it was the Empire Hotel. Not only does Kerouac name the Stevens Hotel by name in two novels, but common sense suggests that a man with a large pack would prefer to walk the three blocks from the ferry terminal to First and Marion rather than trudge the entire length of the waterfront in search of a flop. Besides, in the 1950s the Stevens Hotel, which was built in the nineteenth century, featured a large lighted sign on its roof that would have been as clearly visible to Kerouac from the ferry as the "Port of Seattle" neon he noticed on top of the Bell Street Terminal far to the north. This is not to say that Kerouac never slept in the Jell-O-Mold building, only that his residence there is at present a legend rather than an established fact.

After only one night at the Stevens, where for a dollar and seventy-five cents he got a room, a hot bath, and a good long sleep, Jack headed out. On First Avenue—thrift store fans will be pleased to read—he "found all kinds of Goodwill stores with wonderful sweaters and red underwear for sale." Before hitting the road he "had a big breakfast with five-cent coffee in the crowded market morning with blue sky and clouds scudding overhead and waters of Puget Sound sparkling and dancing under old piers." Relishing his first taste of the "real true Northwest," he packed up his purchases in his rucksack, checked out of the Stevens, and "walked out to 99 a few miles out of town" on June 21, 1956. The palpable excitement of his initial visit pervades these descriptions of Kerouac's first few hours in Seattle.

In *Lonesome Traveler*, a collection of short pieces published in 1960, Kerouac presented his impressions of the city that summer in a paragraph of travelogue that still rings true over forty years later:

> Anybody who's been to Seattle and missed Alaskan Way, the old waterfront, has missed the point—here the totem-pole stores, the waters of Puget Sound washing under old piers, the dark gloomy look of ancient warehouses and pier shed, and the most antique locomotives in America switching boxcars up and down the waterfront, give a hint, under the pure cloud-mopped skies of the Northwest, of great country to come. Driving north from Seattle on Highway 99 is an exciting experience because suddenly you see the Cascade Mountains rising on the northeast horizon, truly Komo

> Kulshan [the Nooksack words for "white, shining, steep mountain," their name for Mount Baker] under their uncountable snows.—The great peaks covered with trackless white, worlds of huge rock twisted and heaped and sometimes almost spiraled into fantastic unbelievable shapes. (*Lonesome Traveler* 119)

Kerouac's lengthy repetition of his experience on Desolation Peak in four different books—accounts presumably all drawn from the same journal—gives some indication of the importance of the spiritual crisis he endured in the course of sixty-three days alone on the mountaintop. In *The Dharma Bums*, where the experience concludes the novel, his description is positively uplifting, while the account of the same period in *Lonesome Traveler* is more detached and reportorial. Taking its title from the mountain peak on which it opens, *Desolation Angels* begins as *The Dharma Bums* ends, but by contrast with the earlier novel it tells a horror story of two months of isolation in which Jack Duluoz, the Kerouac character, ruminating on the anniversary of the deaths of his brother (in 1926) and his father (in 1946), delves deep into his own personality only to find that he hates himself (*Desolation Angels* 61). In the "7th Chorus" of "Desolation Blues" (alluding to Gary Snyder's translation of *Cold Mountain Poems*) he expresses his desperate desire

> to get down
> Off this Chinese Han Shan hill
> and make it
> To the city & walk the streets
> And drink good wine (*Book of Blues* 123)

Needless to say, his mood on returning to Seattle is tinged by his sense of relief at having survived his dark night of the soul and arrived safely back in society.

Thanks to a factual reference in *Desolation Angels* we can ascertain the exact date of Kerouac's return: Wednesday, September 12, 1956. You may have noticed in the passages I quoted previously that Kerouac tends both to identify those features of the landscape that have personal meaning—such as the switch engines on the docks—and to universalize the scene as somehow symbolic of all America. He continues to follow this practice on his return trip, when his ride to town drops him off near the University of Washington campus, which he dismisses as "all right and pretty Eternal." Wasting no time on the "all right" college scene, Jack takes "the first bus into downtown Seattle" (*Desolation Angels* 101), calling into question the factual basis of the legend of his regular drinking at the Blue Moon on 45th Street. Downtown he finds

> ...old ships of sea water with ancient scows in em, and red sun sinks behind the masts and shedrooves, that's better, I understand that, it's old Seattle of the fog, old Seattle the city in the shroud, old Seattle I'd read about as a kid in Blue Books for Men all about the old days a hundred men breaking into the embalmer's cellar and drinking embalming fluid and all dying, and all being Shanghaied to China that way...the Seattle of ships—ramps—clocks—totem poles—old locomotives switching on the waterfront—steam, smoke—Skid Row, bars—Indians—the Seattle of my boyhood vision I see there in rusted old junkyard with old non color fence leaning in a general maze. (*Desolation Angels* 101)

Kerouac's own account of his second visit continues in this way:

> I go all the way down to First Avenue and turn left, leaving the shoppers and the Seattleites behind, and lo! here's all humanity hep and weird wandering on the evening sidewalk amazing me outa my eyeballs—Indian girls in slacks, with Indian boys with Tony Curtis haircuts—twisted—arm in arm—families of old Okie fame just parked their car in the lot, going down to the market for bread and meat—Drunks—The doors of bars I fly by incredible with crowded sad waiting humanity, fingering drinks and looking up at the Johnny Saxton-Carmen Basilio fight on TV—And bang! I realize it's Friday night all over America.... (*Desolation Angels* 101–102)

In fact, the Saxton-Basilio rematch, in which Carmen Basilio recaptured the world welterweight championship with a TKO in the ninth round, was a Wednesday night fight, but Kerouac transposes it in order to evoke the characteristic American excitement at the beginning of the weekend, the same time as he had set *Old Angel Midnight*: "Friday afternoon in the universe" (1). Kerouac goes into a bar, sets his pack down on the floor, and orders a beer. Watching the bout, he identifies with the loser's brains and attributes to the other patrons Basilio's guts. Realizing that their drinking may ultimately lead to a barroom brawl in imitation of the televised fight, he warns himself:

"You gotta be a nutty wild masochistic Johnny O New York to go to Seattle and take up fistfighting in bars!" (*Desolation Angels* 103). Immediately, he makes a haiku-like resolution:
>A night in Seattle.
>Tomorrow, the road to Frisco.

After again paying $1.75 for a night in the same Stevens Hotel and getting settled in his room, Duluoz, taking up a poignant theme explored in both *The Dharma Bums* and *Desolation Angels* and continued in the twelve choruses of "Desolation Blues," pauses a moment for a Buddhist reflection on what he has just seen:

>Ah Seattle, sad faces of the human bars, and you don't realize you're upsidedown—Your sad heads, people, hang down in the unlimited void, you go skipplering around the surface of streets and even in rooms, upsidedown, your furniture is upsidedown and held by gravity, the only thing prevents it from all flying off is the laws of the mind of the universe, God—.... (*Desolation Angels* 103)

As he often does, Kerouac moves rapidly from the sublime to the ridiculous. In a shop where he has gone to buy a *Sporting News* and a copy of *Time* to catch up on events in the world he has been absent from for over two months, he remarks on the racks full of "a thousand girlie books" *(Desolation Angels* 103). Naturally, he finds that he is extremely horny, and on the way back to his room to read he passes a burlesque house and resolves to spend the evening there. This was probably the Rivoli, "the city's last grand burlesque house" (Paul Dorpat, *1st Ave. $1*, 33), which was still offering live shows in the 1950s on the opposite end of the block from the Stevens Hotel.

As you can well imagine, like most cities Seattle has not been careful to preserve its erotic history. Fortunately, I found an antique dealer on Alaskan Way who had a copy of a brown paper packet sold by the Rivoli Theater in the early 1950s. I have tried to correlate the photos of the strippers with the text of Kerouac's description of his visit to the show, reprinted in 1957 in the *Evergreen Review*, the first of the underground magazines to go mass market (I,4:106–112), and in 1963 in the influential anthology *The Moderns*, edited by LeRoi Jones, as "Seattle Burlesque." To my mind, this is one of Kerouac's best set-pieces:

>Aw, they've got little Sis Merriday up there, girl from across the bay, she oughtnt be dancing in no burlesque, when she shows her

breasts (which are perfect) nobody's interested because she aint thrown out no otay hipwork—she's too clean—the audience in the dark theater, upside down, want a dirty girl—And dirty girl's in back getting upsidedown before her stagedoor mirror—....

(Desolation Angels 105)

They bring her out, the Spanish dancing girl, Lolita from Spain, long black hair and dark eyes and wild castanets and she starts stripping, casting her garments aside with an "Ole!" and a shake of her head and showing teeth, everybody eats in her cream shoulders and cream legs and she whirls around the castanet and comes down with her fingers slowly to her cinch and undoes the whole skirt, underneath's a pretty sequined virginity-belt, with spangles, she jams around and dances and stomps and lowers her haid-hair to the floor and...That Lolita goes slumming around then ends up at the sidedrape revealing her breast-bras but wont take them off....

(*Desolation Angels* 106)

...Seattle's own redhead Kitty O'Grady...she's tall and got green eyes and red hair and minces around...Pretty Miss O'Grady, I can see her bassinets...the beauty spots on her cheek...she tries hard to be naughty but caint, goes off showing her breasts (that take up a whistle)....

(Desolation Angels 107–108)

"And now—the Naughty Girl—Sarina!"...There's a furor of excitement throughout the theater—She has slanted cat's eyes and a wicked face—cute like cat's mustache—like a little witch—she comes slinking and bumping out to the beat....

(*Desolation Angels* 108)

Duluoz, drunk and disappointed by the documentary films that separated the live shows ("Sawmills, dust, smoke, gray pictures of logs splashing in water, men with tin hats wandering in a gray rainy void and the announcer: 'the proud tradition of the Northwest'—then followed by color pictures of waterskiers..." [*Desolation Angels* 110]), staggers into "the outside night air of Seattle, on a hill, by redbrick neons of the stagedoor" and falls into a fit of melancholy, despairing that no girl will want to sleep with such a drunken old bum—he was thirty-four at the time—as himself. To make matters worse, after a quick Chinese dinner, he gets on the elevator back at the hotel with a crippled man escorting a woman to his room, and later Duluoz hears them "creak the bed in the next room in real sexual ecstasy" (*Desolation Angels* 111).

In the morning—presumably Thursday, September 13—complaining of blisters on his feet but not mentioning his probable hangover, Duluoz decides to take the bus to San Francisco flush with his summer pay. Before checking out of the Stevens, however, he trudges up the hill out of Skid Row and finds "a splendid serve-yourself restaurant where you pour your own coffee as many time's you want and pay that on an honor basis and get your bacon and eggs at the counter and eat at tables..." (*Desolation Angels* 113). Nothing testifies to Kerouac's vitality in 1956 better than the power of cheap, simple food to restore his sagging spirits. After checking out of his hotel, Duluoz makes this observation:

> Everything is so keen when you come down from solitude, I notice all Seattle with every step I take—I'm going down the sunny main drag now with pack on back and room rent paid and lotsa pretty girls eating ice cream cones and shopping in the 5 & 10—On one corner I see an eccentric paperseller with a wagon-bike loaded with ancient issues of magazines and bits of string and thread, an oldtime Seattle character "*The Reader's Digest* should write about him," I think, and go to the bus station and buy my ticket to Frisco.
> (*Desolation Angels* 114)

After a brief infatuation with a waitress in a soda fountain near the bus depot—another marvel of compression of detail to create a wistful, romantic mood—Duluoz boards his bus, which pulls out of Seattle and goes barreling south to Portland on swish-swish 99" (*Desolation Angels* 117).

In slightly less than three months in the Northwest, Kerouac spent a mere two days in Seattle, yet those two days impressed themselves indelibly on his writerly imagination as the appropriate frame for his profound experience on Desolation Peak. The Jack Kerouac who returned to the Stevens Hotel on the night of September 12, 1956, was not the same Jack Kerouac who arrived there in mid-June. A complex set of emotional circumstances came together during his two months on the mountaintop, leading to his confrontation with his own internal demons. He had been forced to abandon the illusion, which he had cherished for at least ten years, that like his fellow New Englander Thoreau, he could live a life of solitary meditation. Kerouac needed the excitement of social life more than he needed peace and quiet. Though his nine weeks without drugs or alcohol on Desolation Peak also seem to have convinced him that these substances were unnecessary and even harmful to his spiritual pursuits *(Desolation Angels* 96), he began to drink in desperate earnest when he came down. Less than a year later the publication of *On the Road* thrust Kerouac into the unflattering light of the national media as "The King of the Beatniks." From that moment, which ought to have marked the pinnacle of his long struggle to reach the status of literary artist, it was all downhill, leading to his early death from alcoholism in 1969. Kerouac's visit to the Northwest was the prelude to his fall, and as always in his writing, he managed to record the good, bad, and indifferent moments of his two days in Seattle with a fidelity and vividness that make them symbolic. To this day—and probably for a long time to come—his descriptions of the city resonate with readers around the world because of Kerouac's ability to forge from simple, subjective values a universal truth.

Bibliography

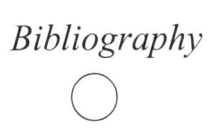

Jack Kerouac's Nine Lives

Works Cited and Consulted

Abbot, H. Porter. "Autobiography, Autography, Fiction: Groundwork for a Taxonomy of Textual Categories." *New Literary History* 19,3 (Spring 1988): 597-615.

Amburn, Ellis. *Subterranean Kerouac: The Hidden Life of Jack Kerouac*. NY: St. Martin's Press, 1998.

—. "You Don't Know Jack." *Out* (August 1998):57-61.

Barthes, Roland. *Mythologies*. NY: Hill and Wang, 1972.

Beaulieu, Victor-Levy. *Jack Kerouac: A Chicken-Essay*. Trans. Sheila Fischman. Toronto: Coach House Press, 1976.

Bent, Jaap van der. "Jack Kerouac and His Biographers: Lost Generation, Beat Generation, Found Generation." *Moody Street Irregulars: A Jack Kerouac Magazine* 14 (Spring 1984): 5-7.

Blue Beat Jacket. Ed. Yusuke Keida. Nos. 1-10 (1993-1996).

Brinkley, Douglas. "In the Kerouac Archive." *Atlantic Monthly* (Nov. 1998): 49-76.

Bruccoli, Mary, ed. "Jack Kerouac" in *Dictionary of Literary Biography Documentary Series:An Illustrated Chronicle, v. 3* (Detroit: Gale, 1983):71-122.

Cassady, Carolyn. *Heartbeat*. Berkeley: Creative Arts, 1976.

—. *Off the Road: My Years with Cassady, Kerouac and Ginsberg*. NY: Morrow, 1990.

Cassady, Neal. *The First Third*. San Francisco: City Lights, 1981.

Challis, Chris. *Quest for Kerouac*. London: Faber & Faber, 1984.

Charters, Ann. "Allen Ginsberg and Jack Kerouac, Columbia Undergraduates." *Columbia Library Columns* 20:1 (Nov. 1970): 10-17.

—. *Beats and Company*.

—. *Jack Kerouac: A Bibliography*. NY: The Phoenix Bookshop, 1975.

—. "Jack Kerouac" in *Dictionary of Literary Biography, v. 2: American Novelists Since WWII* (Detroit: Gale, 1978): 255-261.

—. "Jack Kerouac" in *American Writers: A Collection of Literary Biographies, Supplement III, Part 1* (NY: Scribner's, 1991): 217-234.

—. *Kerouac: A Biography*. NY: St. Martin's, 1994.

—, ed. *The Beats: Literary Bohemians in Postwar America*. Dictionary of Literary Biography, v.16. Detroit: Gale, 1984.

—, ed. *The Portable Jack Kerouac*. NY: Viking/Penguin, 1995.

—, comp. *Scenes Along the Road: Photographs of the Desolation Angels 1944-1960*. San Francisco: City Lights, 1970.

Christy, Jim. *The Long Slow Death of Jack Kerouac*. Toronto: ECW Press, 1998.

Clark, Tom. *Jack Kerouac*. NY: Harcourt, 1984.

—. *Jack Kerouac in San Francisco*. Berkeley: Beat Books, 1983.

Cook, Bruce. *The Beat Generation*. NY: Scribner's, 1971.

Dharma Beat. Ed. Attila Guyenis and Mark Hemenway. Nos. 1-10 (1993-1998).

Dorfner, John J. *Kerouac: Visions of Lowell*. Foreword by Allen Ginsberg. Raleigh, NC: Cooper Street Publications, 1993.

—. *Kerouac: Visions of Rocky Mount*. Raleigh, NC: Cooper Street Publications, 1991.

Edington, Stephen. *Kerouac's Nashua Connection*. Nashua, NH: Transition Publishing, 1999.

Foye, Brian, and Mark Hemenway. *Jack Kerouac's Lowell: A Guide to the Neighborhoods That Shaped Jack Kerouac's Life and Writing*. Lowell: Lowell Celebrates Kerouac! and the Jack Kerouac Subterranean Information Society, (1994?).

Gifford, Barry. *Kerouac's Town*. With photographs by Marshall Clements. Berkeley: Creative Arts Book Co., 1977.

Gifford, Barry, and Lawrence Lee. *Jack's Book: An Oral Biography*. NY: Penguin, 1979.

Ginsberg, Allen. *Visions of the Great Rememberer.* Amherst, MA: Mulch Press, 1974.

Go Moan for Man. Film. Dir. Doug Sharples. 1999.

Grauerholz, James. "A Case Study in Plagiarism." July 1976. (Copy in author's possession.)

Haverty, Joan. *Nobody's Wife.* Berkeley: Creative Arts, 2000.

Heart Beat. Film. Dir. John Byrum. 1979.

Holmes, John Clellon. *Gone in October.* Hailey, Idaho: Limberlost Press, 1985.

—. *Representative Men.* Fayetteville: University of Arkansas Press, 1988.

—. *Visitor in Old Saybrook.* Vol. 2 of *the unspeakable visions of the individual.* California, PA: the unspeakable visions of the individual, 1981.

Huncke, Herbert. *Guilty of Everything.* NY: Paragon, 1990.

Hunt, Tim. Kerouac's *Crooked Road: Development of a Fiction.* Berkeley: University of California Press, 1996.

Jack Kerouac's Road. Film. Dir. Hermenegilde Chiasson. 1987.

Jarvis, Charles. *Visions of Kerouac.* Lowell: Ithaca Press, 1974.

Johnson, Joyce. *Minor Characters.* Boston: Houghton Mifflin, 1983.

—. "Outlaw Days" in The Beats: *Literary Bohemians in Postwar America.* Part II:M-Z. Detroit: Gale, 1984.

Jones, James T. *Use My Name: Jack Kerouac's Forgotten Families.* Toronto: ECW Press, 1999.

Kerouac. Film. Dir. John Antonelli. 1984.

Kerouac: On the Road with Jack. Los Angeles: Active Home Video, 1990.

Kerouac, Jack. "The Art of Fiction." Interview by Ted Berrigan. *The Paris Review* 43 (Summer 1968): 60-105.

—. *Big Sur.* NY: McGraw-Hill, 1962.

—. *Book of Dreams.* San Francisco: City Lights, 1961.

—. *Book of Tics.* Notebook in the Berg Collection, New York City Public Library.

—. "Found Text Series–Jack Kerouac: Letters from Jack Kerouac to Ed White, 1947-68." *The Missouri Review* (1994):107-160.

—. *Jack Kerouac: Selected Letters, 1940-1956*. Ed. Ann Charters. NY: Viking, 1995.

—. *Jack Kerouac: Selected Letters, 1957-1969*. Ed. Ann Charters. NY: Viking, 1999.

—. *Mexico City Blues*. NY: Grove, 1959.

—. *More Mexico City Blues*. Notebook in the Berg Collection, New York City Public Library.

—. "On the Road Again." Ed. Douglas Brinkley. *The New Yorker* (June 22 and 29, 1998):46-59.

—. *Satori in Paris* and *Pic*. NY: Grove, 1981.

—. SK-OB. Notebook in Berg Collection, New York City Public Library.

—. *The Subterraneans*. NY: Grove, 1958.

Kerouac, Stella Sampas. Letter to Ann Charters (22 December 1972) in the Charters Collection now combined with the Berg Collection, New York City Public Library.

Kerouac's Lowell Places—A Guide. Lowell: Lowell City Library, n.d.

The Kerouac Connection. Ed. Dave Moore, James Morton, and Mitchell Smith. Nos. 1-28 (1984–1998).

The Kerouac Quarterly. Ed. Paul Maher. Nos. 1-3 (1996-1998).

Knight, Arthur and Kit, eds. *Kerouac and the Beats: A Primary Sourcebook*. NY: Paragon House, 1988.

Krim, Seymour. "The Kerouac Legacy" in *What's This Cat's Story: The Best of Seymour Krim* (NY: Paragon, 1991):88-104.

The Last Time I Committed Suicide. Film. Dir. Stephen Kay. Starring Keanu Reaves. 1997.

Latham, Aaron. "The Columbia Murder That Gave Birth to the Beats." *New York Magazine* (19 April 1976):41-53.

Lemire, Bernice. *Jack Kerouac: Early Influences*. Master's Thesis, Boston College, 1962.

Lenrow, Elbert. "Memoir: The Young Kerouac." *Narrative* 2,1(Jan. 1994):65-86.

Malcolm, Janet. *The Silent Woman: Sylvia Plath & Ted Hughes*. NY: Knopf, 1994.

Marcus, Greil. *The Dustbin of History*. Cambridge, MA: Harvard University Press, 1995.

McDarrah, Fred W. *Kerouac and Friends: A Beat Generation Album.* NY: William Morrow, 1985.

McNally, Dennis. *Desolate Angel.* NY: Random House, 1979.

Miles, Barry. *Allen Ginsberg: A Biography.* NY: Simon & Schuster, 1989.

—. *El Hombre Invisible: William S. Burroughs.* London: Virgin Publications, 1992.

—. *Jack Kerouac: King of the Beats.* NY: Grove Press, 1998.

Milewski, Robert J. *Jack Kerouac: An Annotated Bibliography of Secondary Sources, 1944-1979.* Metuchen, NJ: Scarecrow Press, 1981.

Montgomery, John. *Jack Kerouac: A Memoir.* Fresno, CA: Giligia Press, 1970.

—, comp. *Kerouac at the "Wild Boar" and Other Skirmishes.* San Anselmo, CA: Fels & Firn Press, 1986.

—, comp. *The Kerouac We Knew: Unposed Portraits; Action Shots.* Kentfield, CA: Fels & Firn Press, 1982.

Moody Street Irregulars. Ed. Joy Walsh. Nos. 1-28 (1978-1994).

Morgan, Bill. *The Beat Generation in New York: A Walking Tour of Jack Kerouac's City.* San Francisco: City Lights, 1997.

Morrow, Bradford, Bookseller. *Catalogue Five.* (1978?)

Nicosia, Gerald. *Memory Babe: A Critical Biography of Jack Kerouac.* NY: Grove Press, 1983.

—. *The Two Lowells of Jack Kerouac.* Coventry, England: Beat Scene Press, 1988.

Parker, Brad. *Kerouac: An Introduction.* Lowell, MA: Lowell Corporation for the Humanities, 1989.

Plummer, William. *The Holy Goof.* NY: Paragon, 1988.

Profile: Jack Kerouac. Video. Bravo, April 1998.

Ronan, Stephen. *Jack Kerouac, Recording Artist.* Berkeley: Ammunition Press, 1997.

Sampas, Sebastian. Letter to William Saroyan. (Copy in author's possession.)

Shuttleworth, Charles, comp. *Portals of Possibility: Kerouac at Horace Mann, 1939-'40.* Draft ms. 17 May 1994, including copies of the *Horace Mann Record.* (Copies in the author's possession.)

Smith, Dinitia. "Scholars and Survivors Tatter Kerouac's Self-Portrait." *The New York Times* (9 July 1998): EI,E4.

Strachey, Lytton. *Eminent Victorians*. NY: Harcourt Brace, 1969.

Suarez, Ray. *Talk of the Nation* (April 1998). National Public Radio interview with Douglas Brinkley, Ann Charters, Joyce Johnson, and John Sampas.

The Subterraneans. Film. Dir. Ranald MacDougall. 1960.

Turner, Steve. *Jack Kerouac: Angelheaded Hipster*. NY: Viking, 1996.

Vidal, Gore. *Palimpsest: A Memoir*. NY: Random House, 1995.

Wakefield, Dan. *New York in the Fifties*. Boston: Houghton Mifflin/Seymour Lawrence, 1992.

Watson, Steven. *The Birth of the Beat Generation: Visionaries, Rebels, and Hipsters, 1944-1960*. NY: Pantheon, 1995.

What Happened to Kerouac? Film. Dir. Richard Lerner and Lewis MacAdams. 1986.

White, Michael, ed. *Safe in Heaven Dead*. NY: Hanuman, 1990.

Kerouactonyms

Works Cited and Consulted

Cassady, Carolyn. *Off the Road: My Years with Cassady, Kerouac and Ginsberg*. NY: Morrow, 1990.

Challis, Chris. "An Unauthorized Change in Jack Kerouac's *The Dharma Bums*?" *Notes on Modern American Literature* (Autumn 1982): item 13.

Cook, Bruce. *The Beat Generation*. NY: Scribners, 1971.

Davenport, Steven. *Complicating "a very masculine aesthetic": Positional Sons and Double Husbands, Kinship and Careening in Jack Kerouac's Fiction*. Univ. of Illinois Dissertation, 1992.

Foster, Edward H. *Understanding the Beats*. Columbia: U of South Carolina P, 1992.

French, Warren. *Jack Kerouac*. Boston: G. K. Hall, 1986.

Gifford, Barry, and Lawrence Lee. *Jack's Book: An Oral Biography of Jack Kerouac*. NY: Penguin, 1979.

Ginsberg, Allen. *Collected Poems 1947-1984*. NY: Harper & Row, 1984.

Goddard, Dwight, ed. *A Buddhist Bible*. Boston: Beacon, 1983.

Harrington, Alan. *The Secret Swinger*. NY: Knopf, 1966.

Hipkiss, Robert A. *Jack Kerouac: Prophet of the New Romanticism*. Lawrence, Kansas: The Regents Press of Kansas, 1976.

Hochman, Baruch. *Character in Literature*. Ithaca: Cornell UP, 1985.

Huncke, Herbert. *Guilty of Everything*. NY: Paragon House, 1990.

Hunt, Tim. *Kerouac's Crooked Road: Development of a Fiction*. Hampden, Connecticut: Archon, 1981.

Jarvis, Charles. *Visions of Kerouac*. Lowell, MA: Ithaca Press, 1974.

Johnson, Joyce. *Minor Characters*. Boston: Houghton, Mifflin, 1983.

Kerouac, Jack. *Big Sur*. NY: McGraw, 1981.
—. *Book of Dreams*. San Francisco: City Lights, 1961.
—. *Desolation Angels*. NY: Putnam's, 1980.
—. *The Dharma Bums*. NY: Viking Penguin, 1976.
—. *Dr. Sax: Faust Part Three*. NY: Grove, 1975.
—. *Good Blonde and Others*. San Francisco: Grey Fox, 1996.
—. *Mexico City Blues*. NY: Grove, 1959.
—. *On the Road*. NY: Viking Penguin, 1992.
—. *Satori in Paris* and *Pic*. NY: Grove, 1985.
—. *Selected Letters of Jack Kerouac, 1940-1956*. Ed. Ann Charters. NY: Viking, 1995.
—. *The Subterraneans*. NY: Grove, 1981.
—. *The Town and the City*. NY: Harcourt, 1983.
—. *Vanity of Duluoz: An Adventurous Education, 1935-46*. London: Quartet, 1975.
—. *Visions of Cody*. NY: McGraw, 1974.
Rigney, Francis J., and L. Douglas Smith. *The Real Bohemia: A Sociological and Psychological Study of the "Beats."* NY: Basic Books, 1961.
Salinger, J. D. *Nine Stories*. Boston: Little, Brown, 1953.
Sandison, David. *Jack Kerouac: An Illustrated Biography*. Chicago: Chicago Review Press, 1999.
Yeats, William Butler. *The Collected Poems of W. B. Yeats*. NY: Macmillan, 1983.

Other Books by Jim Jones

◯

A Map of Mexico City Blues: Jack Kerouac as Poet
Southern Illinois University Press, 1992
ISBN   0-8093-1828-8

The Paradox of Spontaniety
Elbow Press, 1995
2225 1st Ave. #206
Seattle, WA 98121

Jack Kerouac's Duluoz Legend:
The Mythic Form of an Autobiographical Fiction
Southern Illinois University Press, 1999
ISBN 0-8093-2263-3

Use My Name: Jack Kerouac's Forgotten Families
ECW Press, 1999
ISBN2 1-55022-375-5